BLACK VICTIM
TO
BLACK VICTOR

- SECOND EDITION -

IDENTIFYING THE IDEOLOGIES, BEHAVIORAL PATTERNS AND CULTURAL NORMS THAT ENCOURAGE A VICTIMHOOD COMPLEX

ADAM B. COLEMAN

SECOND EDITION EDITED BY DR. TANYA HETTLER

Wrong Speak Publishing LLC

PO Box 8323

Piscataway, NJ 08854

www.wrongspeak.net

promotions@wrongspeak.net

ISBN 979-8-9893957-5-0

Second Edition

10 9 8 7 6 5 4 3 2

- ACKNOWLEDGEMENTS -

Since the original publishing of this book, the support I've gained has been far beyond my expectations. I'm incredibly thankful for all my supporters and industry colleagues for their grace.

I continue to praise my amazing wife Michele for being my unwavering support system and without her love, grace and encouragement, I don't believe I would have been able to accomplish nearly as much as I've been able to in my life.

You don't often find individuals who believe in you from the first time they meet you and are willing to not only be your friend but also a mentor: Batya Ungar-Sargon is a rare kind soul in a harsh world. I cannot thank her enough for everything she's done to support me in my career, and I hold immense gratitude for being able to call her my friend.

I appreciate the continued love that my entire family has shown me, and I cannot thank them enough for blessing me with their support.

This second edition would not have happened if it weren't for God putting Dr. Tanya Hettler in my life to help me edit and improve this book.

As the first edition was dedicated to my only child and son who was a boy witnessing the growth of his father and learning how to become a man himself, I continue to dedicate this book to the adult man he is today.

Words cannot describe how proud I am of him, and I am blessed to witness his pride in me throughout this journey. I speak out partly because I want to be an example for my son and show that he should not be afraid to speak his mind because restricting your voice hurts more than the repercussions of vocalizing an alternate and genuine perspective.

I'd like to thank God for gracing me with the strength to overcome my pain, fear, and anxiety to become the man I am today.

This book is in loving memory of my Aunt Anne who is now embraced in God's loving arms in Heaven.

- TABLE OF CONTENTS -

- INTRODUCTION -

QUESTIONS

Am I actually broken and if I am broken, can I be fixed? Why did it feel as if my birth created an inconvenience for my father and a burden for my mother? Why is the choice of neglect commonplace for black men? Why are black women excused for failing to select better men?

Why am I told to distrust the white man when I couldn't even depend on my black father? If the greatest danger to a black man in America is the white man, then why do the most successful black people choose to live in white neighborhoods? Why should my pigmentation determine my aspirations? Why must I live in the past with the pain of my ancestors instead of creating a future of hope?

Why does wanting aspirations of racial togetherness make me a traitor? Why is Martin Luther King Jr. given hero status, but we never listen to our hero's message? Why is forgiveness seen as a weakness and resentment seen as empowerment? Why is white supremacy bad and black supremacy good? Why is hatred seen as subjective instead of objective?

Why must black people fit in a box? Why aren't we allowed to decide for ourselves? Why must I fit a narrative? Why do we focus on race instead of class? Why does everyone think that they need to help black people? Why are black people tolerating lowered expectations imposed by the leftist elite? Why must black people be America's charity case?

How can we expect more from other Americans when we don't appear to expect much from ourselves? Why do we stay quiet when black men terrorize the innocent within our communities but speak loudly when one of these terrorists dies? Why do we make martyrs out of flawed black men and ignore honorable black men? Why are a third of our pregnant black women aborting their children?

Why do we wait for the government to save us when we are capable of saving ourselves? Why do we overlook the destructive role that the government has played in our community since the beginning? Why have we allowed family court to displace the black family? Why have we reduced the importance of the black father to a bi-weekly check? Who is benefitting from our familial disorder?

Could it be that the political elite that find us more controllable divided than united? Could it be the alleged black leadership that needs useful victims for their boundless greed? Why are black people the only racial group that is expected to have authority figures? Why is it that these so-called black leaders are always in bed with the political establishment?

Why is honest curiosity seen as an assault? Why do these questions offend you? Why am I not given the benefit of the doubt? Why does removing black victimhood make us feel naked? Why are excuses replacing actions and intentions replacing results? Why are we not willing to admit that there has been immense progress made? Is it because we are secretly afraid of losing our leverage over white guilt?

Are we more in love with complaining than repairing? Do we believe we can achieve prosperity without the help of anyone else? Do we want to be America's perpetual victim, or do we want to become America's resilient victors?

These are only some questions I've asked myself since I was a child. Much about black culture has always made me ask "Why?" This book is my attempt to answer these questions as thoughtfully and honestly as possible. I know I'm not the only person who has thought about some of these questions, but we are generally unwilling to talk about them publicly.

Within this book, I will critique a variety of taboo areas and you must understand that these critiques do not stem from hatred, they stem from concern. I will not attack people, I will attack the ideologies, behavioral patterns and culture that surround us all. We can change the way we think and behave if we are willing to be honest and clear in our analysis and I've spent countless hours carefully crafting this message.

This book is not about converting people. Frankly, we spend too much time trying to convert people to have them think the way we do instead of just supplying a different perspective. I do not expect everyone that reads this book to agree with everything I state. But if this book gets you to question at least one of your previously held beliefs, then I have achieved my goal. I want people to question things more in their life, question the world around them and be lovingly critical when doing so.

I wrote this book passionately because I wanted to express a message of love while talking about some tough topics. If you at any point during your reading experience begin to believe that I have hatred or anger about a group of people, then I would ask that you stop reading until you clear this notion from your mind. Too many of us have been corrupted with passive hatred and it is easy to misinterpret criticisms as being hate, but that is not me and that is not my intention.

There are valid questions that need to be asked and answered. Without these questions, black Americans will continue to be in a mental state of victimhood in America when I truly believe that we can be victors. The first step to answering these questions is to be uncomfortably honest with ourselves and the world around us. In doing so, it will remove the gap in honesty that currently prevails.

- CHAPTER 1 -

A GAP IN HONESTY

"The ultimate measure of a man is not where he stands in moments of comfort and convenience, but where he stands at times of challenge and controversy."

– Dr. Martin Luther King Jr.

"Strength of Love"

1963

Far too often we are afraid to be honest with ourselves because the truth seems offensive. We purposely hide from reality because it hurts our good-natured sensibilities. But in many cases, this avoidance hurts us by allowing us to maintain a false view of reality. We promote ideologies and policies based on lies that make us feel good but hold no real-world value. When there is an obvious problem, we focus on the symptom because the problem is disturbingly too real.

In America, we have a glaringly obvious gap in honesty when we talk about culture and race but not in the way that you may think. I am talking about the reality of cultural differences, not racial differences. We are glued to race because the discussion of racism is superficially easy, but discussions around cultural differences are extremely taboo. Anytime someone attempts to talk about culture, it automatically gets redirected back to race like an American reflex. I want to dive into the uncomfortable in this book by discussing culture, ideology, psychology, and a variety of other uncomfortable areas that too many people avoid for fear of being slandered as something they are not.

Here is a simple exercise to examine how honest we are: If a woman is walking through a parking garage alone at night and hears a man walking 20 feet behind her, should she not be worried? It would not be irrational for her to be slightly worried or at the very least aware. Does her being worried make her some anti-male feminist? Of course not. She should have legitimate concern because the reality is that, unfortunately, some men rape women and men on average are stronger than women, decreasing the chances of her defending herself without a weapon. Now, say it is me, a black man, walking behind her. Should she still be worried? The answer is yes, because I am still a man and yes, because I am black.

It is uncomfortable to admit these numbers, but they are part of the truth that shows that there is a legitimate problem. Black Americans account for about 13% of the U.S. population and black men account for about 6% of the population. FBI statistics from 2019 show that the 6% black male demographic account for about 51% of the murder arrests, 52% of robbery arrests and 26% of rape arrests. These are high percentages for such a small demographic, especially when compared to the white male demographic, which is about 31% of the U.S. population.

It gives me no pleasure to state this, in fact, it saddens me that this is the truth. But hiding from it due to discomfort does not help. Obviously, black men are not inherently violent, so there must be a multitude of factors that are contributing to these statistical truths including culture, family, mental health, and societal influences.

We all make the best assumptions in a particular situation based on the information we know. We know that a tiny percentage of the American population commits a significant percentage of the violent crimes, and it is not completely unreasonable for people to be somewhat fearful of this population. Fear is different from hatred and awareness is different from avoidance.

For the situation involving the woman in the parking garage, the truth is that she is not irrational nor is it hateful for her to assume a potential negative outcome because there is some validity in her perception of danger due to my sex and race. It does not make it right, it just makes it the reality. No one enjoys being prejudged but in moments requiring snap judgments, you make the best decision for yourself and your family which is logical.

A couple of years ago, in preparation to leave the country, I ordered a nice shirt online and arranged to have it delivered to my house. The day of the delivery I noticed that I did not receive the package. At this point I checked my account and found that I had accidentally shipped it to an old address where I had not lived for many years. By the time I realized this, it was evening, but I figured I would drive there and hopefully the package would be outside for me to grab and head home.

This neighborhood that I used to live in was considerably upper middle class and relatively quiet. When I lived there, we were the only black people on this street, but we experienced no issues while living there. As I pulled up to my old condo, I noticed that there was no package outside and when presented with no other options: I took a chance and rang the doorbell.

"Who is it?!" a fearful white female voice shouted. She refused to open the door and instead peaked part of her face through the side glass window next to it. I explained that I accidentally shipped a package here because I used to live at this location years ago and the tracking information shows that it says it was delivered today. I politely asked if she received a package with someone else's name on it. She stated she received no package, but she would also admit she never checked her mailbox. I apologized kindly and explained my situation to her, but it felt more like an interrogation. She questioned whether I had ever actually lived at this condo which puzzled me. So, I told her the layout of the inside of the condo to see if that made her feel more at ease, but this tactic did not work.

I could feel her fear even through the door. I am relatively intuitive and once I felt her fear I acknowledged it with her. I empathized by saying, "Listen, I know I'm some stranger and I know you are scared. I just wanted to get my package. I'm going to leave you my information and if you come across it, please contact me." I went to my car to find a pen and piece of paper to write my contact information. When I returned to the door, she was not there, so I rang the doorbell one more time to let her know I was leaving my information outside her door. Suddenly I heard her say "If you ring the bell again, I'm calling the police." at which point I apologized and told her my intentions were to leave my information outside her door and I assured her I was leaving her home.

The next day around noon, I received a text message from an unknown number. The message stated she was the woman I spoke to the day before and she had my package, which was in fact in her mailbox. I explained all I wanted was my package and she could leave it outside with no interaction needed. She followed through by leaving the package outside her home, and I kept my side of the bargain by never contacting her again.

This situation was extremely tense, and I have thought about it in its entirety numerous times. At first, I felt that she acted this way because I was black and maybe she was afraid of black people. I examined my response to the situation and went to the superficially easy claim of racial bias.

But as time went on, I thought about it from her perspective. She was at home relaxing when an unknown black man rang her doorbell at night, claiming that he used to live there, and that he had a package sent there. Even if it were me as a grown black man, I would say this sounds like bullshit and that it is likely an attempt to get me to open the door so they can rob me.

I also considered that she lives in a majority white area and this is a black person who she has never seen before giving a story that seems semi-fictional. I would later consider that because of the criminality of someone that fits my demographic, black male under the age of 40, plus the presence of a story that seems at best odd, she made the most intelligent move possible.

Though I know my intentions were not nefarious, she had no idea who I was and all she could do was rely on the information that she had presented in front of her. With all these details considered, I do not blame this woman for her reaction, nor do I want to chastise her. If she were my wife in the same situation, I would suggest that she not open the door either.

If I am capable of understanding these realities and being honest with myself about the perceived danger of the situation based on many factors, why can't others do the same? Maybe our perception of racism is a misunderstanding of other people and an unfamiliarity with people of other cultures and not necessarily due to race.

When you know your neighbor, you tend not to dislike him, but humans are tribal by nature and we tend to live and interact with primarily our own tribe. In this case, I'm referring to race, but it could also be people of the same political ideology or it could be people of the same occupation and so on.

When we interact with people that we are unfamiliar with, it's normal to be skeptical and somewhat withdrawn. The challenge is looking for a commonality, which provides a giant step forward in personal interactions. I could have easily felt slighted by the harshness of this white woman's voice and held onto my momentary victimhood, but I chose to look deeper into understanding why it all happened in the manner that it did.

I mentioned before that we are reflexive to blame race for many problems in America. But our focus should instead be directed towards culture, more specifically, mainstream black culture. It is a culture riddled with victimhood, bad behavioral habits, glorification of criminality and excuses for all the above. It is this very black culture that is promoted daily within black and white media as fun and edgy, but it is destroying the progress of black America. It is a culture that masks intelligence, responsibility and other positive traits as "white features" while flaunting ignorance, depravity, criminality and degeneracy.

I want to make clear that I will not excuse racism in any form. However, I will not be blind to the obviousness of how culture affects groups of people or how culture alters our perception of racial interactions. When you have a race of people that are dying for some sort of cultural acknowledgment due to a series of negative historical factors, they may slide towards unfortunate tendencies to achieve this. While this negative slide may make sense, it is unreasonable to expect people from other races or cultures to ignore these details.

Let us continue to look honestly at this situation. If you had enough money to move into any neighborhood in America, would you move into a majority black neighborhood or a majority white neighborhood? You would likely choose a white neighborhood and you would probably choose this neighborhood for common sense reasons like better economic opportunities, lower crime rates and greater societal comforts. These are common sense practices for people of all races.

Even black people with economic freedom choose not to reside in black majority ghettos as it would be idiocy to do otherwise. If black neighborhoods were safer than white neighborhoods, everyone would be trying to live amongst blacks, but the reality is that this is not the case. When you look across America, city or town, the least safe neighborhoods tend to have a black majority and the neighborhoods with the least economic opportunities tend to have a black majority; this is fairly obvious.

These are racial realities that we have to first acknowledge before we can start analyzing why this is the case. Black people are not inherently dangerous, yet we live amongst danger and take part in dangerous activity at a higher rate than any other racial group. If our skin color is not the determining factor, then the most obvious reason must be our subscribed cultural standards.

I can already hear the excuses coming my direction, like poverty and racism. But being poor has nothing to do with your moral standards and racism should not stop your pursuit of betterment. The accepted mainstream black culture has been hammered into the minds of many black people for decades due to a communal victim indoctrination and media propaganda which have poisoned us into believing that we have no agency and that we cannot have consistent moral standards because of our economic situation.

Black people are told not to focus on culture because once we do, we will see that there is something gravely wrong with how we think of ourselves and what we are willing to tolerate. We will realize that we are not weak animalistic beings who are hyper-violent, hyper-sexual and helpless in a white majority society. Although there have been outside forces that have contributed to the decline of black culture, we are ultimately responsible for accepting this downfall as our truth.

It would be incorrect to say that every black American subscribes to this cultural shift. However, this gap in honesty is resulting in the narrowing of our prosperity due to the larger acceptance of this conceptual black culture. Even if someone is not participating in the toxic forms of black American culture, like thuggery, addiction and indiscriminate sexual activity, we feel beholden to our race so that we begin to accept or excuse these behaviors.

Blacks in America have always had an element of criminality just like any other racial group in any other society. However, people within most groups chastise those that make everyone else look bad. If that group had a general acceptance of cultural norms within their region, they were likely to abide by them and self-police within their communities. Those who refused to follow these cultural norms would become social pariahs and be consistently disavowed so that others outside the group would not think that one person's bad behavior represented everyone within the group.

We have lost the ability to self-police, self-criticize and reject negative cultural norms because we have become so prideful in areas where we should not be proud. By losing this self-criticism we have become dishonest with ourselves and the world around us. Our pride creates excuses for those who should be ostracized, and once we make excuses for them, we normalize their behavior. What makes it worse is that we would rather believe a comfortable lie than an uncomfortable truth because the truth wounds our sensibilities.

For example, how many unarmed black people do you believe are shot by the police? Hundreds? Thousands? The truth is far fewer than you probably would believe. If I told you that in 2020, the year of massive riots and protests nationwide revolving around the narrative of the abundance of unarmed black killings, that there were only 18 unarmed black people shot and killed by the police, would you believe me? Would you be surprised that in 2019 that there were even fewer killings of unarmed black men, 12 to be exact? The Washington Post has a database of police shootings, I encourage you to look for yourself.

If your reaction to these numbers is a "yeah, but…" then you are letting your pride blind you from the truth. The taking of a life by the state is a tragedy in itself and no one is excusing this, but these numbers should be good news for black Americans.

If this information is not good news to you, then you are more comfortable feeling like a victim than being someone who is in tune with reality. The fact is that there were more people who died from lightning strikes in America (20) than unarmed black people shot and killed by the police in 2020.

This information should be good news in many ways. This means we can stop lying to our young black men when we tell them that they are being targeted by an oppressive white officer who is having a bad day. This means that we can stop living in fear that today might be our last day due to an overzealous police officer.

If this information were known by the majority of black Americans, would it change anything, or would we be too prideful to admit that we were wrong? Would we even be able to acknowledge these facts when leftists are infatuated with and keep pushing the idea of blacks being an endangered species within America?

In a study published by the Skeptic Research Center, they asked people of different political leanings, ranging from very leftist to very conservative, how many black men they thought were killed in 2019? The results showed how astonishingly inaccurate people's perceptions are in relation to the facts. Forty-four percent of these self-described leftists believed that the police killed 1,000 or more unarmed black men. But to be fair, 20% of conservatives thought it was 1,000 or more as well. How can black people move forward when truthful information never seems to come to light? What if everyone knew that the mainstream narrative was a farce? Would we be too prideful to move on to a narrative that is more realistic and likely to produce success?

Throughout my life I have encountered many prideful people, and what I noticed that they had in common was that they were dishonest with themselves. They created this entitlement to be prideful while simultaneously having no real reason for this pride. Prideful people tend to be self-centered and feel a level of importance over others, even though there is no reason for them to feel important. All of this pride manifests itself in dishonest behavior, creating a deceitful societal mask.

The gap in honesty with ourselves is in part due to our pride, but it is a misplaced pride. There are certainly areas of pride that black Americans can grab ahold of but year after year we ignore those positive traits and latch onto negative ones. We used to encourage traditional American traits but they are now dismissed as *white* American traits and thus are rejected. The glue that held us together as Americans as a whole is melting away before our eyes, yet it alarms no one.

In July 2020, the National Museum of African American History & Culture published on their website a poster titled "Aspects & Assumptions of Whiteness & White Culture". They captioned the image by stating "Since white people still hold most of the institutional power in America, we have all internalized some aspects of white culture–including people of color." What are these aspects of "whiteness"? The nuclear family, objective and rational linear thinking, hard work as a key to

20

success, respecting authority, following rigid time schedules, planning for the future, delayed gratification, individualism and the list goes on.

This propaganda is extremely Euro-centric, as if time, or hard work never existed before Europeans. And this is coming from a museum dedicated to the historical documentation of black Americans. Yet it sounds like white supremacist propaganda! It puts whites above blacks and says that all the traits that generally lead to prosperous living are characteristic of the white man. If these traits are white, then the antithesis must be that black traits revolve around us being incapable of rational thinking, lazy, irreverent toward authority, always late, spontaneous, and collectivists. To me this sounds incredibly insulting. The problem is that some black people actually believe this. It is generally enforced with racial shaming, claiming that you are simply "acting white" if you display these characteristics.

The narrative of success has changed so that we question someone's legitimacy as a black person the higher they climb the economic ladder. The implication that equates blackness with poverty and whiteness with wealth only continues our substandard cultural way of thinking and living.

Black Americans have accepted their lower-class citizen status to avoid looking at our own contribution to this status. Criticizing yourself or your own group is a loving trait. Yet we do not love ourselves enough to point out our own cultural flaws. It is painful to highlight areas of imperfection within mainstream black culture, but that is the only way to move closer to prosperity.

Once we become critical of ourselves, we have no choice but to do something about it. Once we see that our kitchen is dirty, we will become responsible for cleaning it. Because we are not honest with ourselves, we are unable to see our own responsibility and it leaves everyone else responsible for our destiny. We disable ourselves all for the sake of comfortable dishonesty which continues our downward spiral. If honesty is love, then dishonesty is hate.

Our public and private positions are sometimes different. We visibly shake our head when we see another crime committed by someone with our complexion, but we just move on and pretend that it is just an isolated incident and not a representation of something foul smelling within black culture. We dare not speak out loud so that others outside the black community can hear our disdain, so we keep it to ourselves. We tread lightly when we talk within our community because we do not want to be seen as traitors. So we remain dishonest and the behavior continues. We know how crazy the hood is, but we refuse to connect it with our accepted culture because that would indict ourselves as part of the problem.

Dishonesty can be hateful because it can lead to believing falsehoods for the sake of someone else's agenda. Without dishonesty, how could we continue to blame white Americans for all of our problems? Without dishonesty, how could we blame all institutions for our lack of progress? Most importantly, without dishonesty, how could we explain why it appears that it is only us with this victim mindset?

I fully recognize how difficult it is to stare someone in the face whom you care about and preach loving honesty. And it is even more daunting to attempt this same act publicly towards a group of people. It takes a bit of bravery and sacrifice of your own personal well-being to stand and speak truth, especially within your own tribe. Thus very few people attempt it and even fewer attempt it and get away unscathed.

When we march in the name of a martyred urban terrorist, the gap widens. When we make excuses for ignorant behavior all for racial preservation, the gap widens. When we feed into a growing culture of depravity, the gap widens. We cannot change what we don't acknowledge. But acknowledgment has to start with ourselves first before we can include anyone else in our call for honesty. We know the truth, but it is embarrassing to acknowledge that we are our own worst enemy.

If each racial group in America had a public relations department, black American's should have been fired a long time ago. We make ourselves look bad by supplying complaints that have no realistic resolutions. When we are angry, we excuse destruction. We rummage through old quotes from black revolutionaries to give legitimacy for our present-day riotous behavior. All because we feel the need to have public temper tantrums that do nothing but destroy our neighborhoods and progress. The empathy we think we are creating will eventually backfire, making it harder to reach the destination that we claim to want to aspire towards.

Our public relations department has failed us by denying reality and clutching onto victimhood to accrue more social currency, but it's a terrible strategy. If social cohesion is the goal, respect will get us to this point, not pity. We have let black activists, intelligentsia and the elite leftist class destroy how the public views black people by leading with dishonesty.

Despite the issues we have as a group, we are progressing in a variety of ways, but that progress is constantly stunted by the profiteers of victimhood. These loud manipulative people fill our television and computer screens daily, denying the social progress that has been made to keep their lucrative industry going. For these men and women, without black suffering, there is no profit.

I have grown up in a dishonest culture and have fought this dishonesty for most of my life. A culture filled with habitually terrible racial concepts and monolithic thoughts of black empowerment. A culture of boxing in black people with restrictive attitudes instead of freeing thoughts. A culture of victim superiority as a supposed reflex to historical white superiority. It is also a culture that is far too comfortable utilizing mafioso tactics against black people who speak about the importance of the nuclear family.

We have to be honest about what is going on around us. The black family has been decimated. Our black cities are war torn. Our black men are denigrated by the women that created them. Our black women have become masculinized to their own detriment. We act selfishly as we are unwilling to sacrifice. We claim to believe in God's word, but consistently fail to live by it. We praise the ignorant and disregard the intelligent. We close our eyes when our body count rises unless it's inflicted by someone of the Caucasian persuasion. Worst of all, we have chosen to stay silent about the voluntary genocide of our unborn.

I do not intend for this book to hurt black Americans. On the contrary, my goal is to help black Americans. The criticisms I will levy throughout this book will always be from a place of love and concern, not rejection. At no point will I distance myself from black America because I am a product of the culture in a variety of ways.

I will use words like "we" constantly throughout this book because I also need to do my part and I am also part of this equation. Before you read on, understand that my criticisms are not about individuals, they are about the ideologies, psychology and behavioral patterns that people live by. Criticizing the ideas that people subscribe to allows room for people to change. Criticizing people relegates them to being immutably flawed.

- CHAPTER 2 -

THE BROKEN BLACK FATHER

"The best parent is both parents" means mommy is no substitute for daddy, money is no substitute for daddy, and another man is no substitute for daddy. Just as daddy is no substitute for mommy, money is no substitute for mommy, and another woman is no substitute for mommy.

–Dr. Warren Farrell

"The Boy Crisis: Why Our Boys Are Struggling and What We Can Do about It"

(2018)

The missing black father is the broken black man who we expect little from, but who we need to help change the destiny of black America. The description of the broken black man as one who experiences hurdles is not to make him as a victim, but to highlight the obstructions that lay in front of him. The control that black women have over the black family is, in part, due to the lack of resilience that is found in many of our black men.

The modern black man has unfortunately been feminized, about which he complains, rather than overcomes. The broken black man has become a defeatist excuse maker whenever his faults are highlighted. If a black woman obstructs him from seeing his child, he may give up rather than standing firm with resilience. These men may also see nothing wrong with giving up because their fathers probably gave up on them as well, perpetuating the cycle of neglect for another generation.

The responsibility black women have, with respect to selecting a suitable father, must be reciprocated. Black men have the responsibility to pursue a woman of substance who would be a suitable mother, rather than entertaining his fetish for female sexual comfort. Men have the responsibility to not only look out for themselves, but their potential offspring, based on the decisions they make. We have a society that caters to the mother by default; black men must be aware of the risk they take when they place short-term pleasure over long-term responsibility.

The broken black father who decides to ignore his fatherly obligation is the epitome of a weak man and deserves little sympathy. Nobody, including other men, respects a weak man. His display of weakness is contagious when it is the example for the black boy. It is the recklessness of the broken black father that not only ruins his own life but his son's life, which is unforgivable.

I can speak harshly of this type of man because my father was this man. No one made him cheat on his wife with my mother, and no one forced him to bear two children outside of his marriage. Yet he chose to discard us rather than care for us. He chose child support payments over personal time with his children. There was never any strength or determination to see his children because he had no interest in making us a part of his life. The broken black man by nature is selfish and egotistical, much like my father, who saw himself as the most important part of the equation rather than acting selflessly, like a responsible father would.

My father chose the simplest and laziest option a father could choose in reaction to having a child - doing nothing. I have thought countless times about how I feel about my father and the one word that constantly comes to mind is "weak". He was too weak a man to fight his sexual urges and stay faithful in his marriage. He was too weak a man to not involve himself in our lives for fear of hurting the marriage he betrayed with his infidelity. He was too weak a man to admit his mistakes to his children and apologize for the pain he inflicted by his absence.

My father wasn't poor. In fact, he did well for himself as a tailor and a business owner. Yet he allowed his children to go in and out of homelessness while my mother was left to pick up the pieces. The nights sitting in a homeless shelter were never followed by a phone call from my father to help financially or give emotional support. We suffered due to the silence from our father and the most minimal effort could have changed our trajectory. Yet he remained apathetic and absent.

The last time I spoke with my father I was 21 years old and it was over the phone. My son was born just months earlier, and I was at a pivotal point in my life. I wanted to make one more attempt at having my father in my life and see if he could overcome his weak-minded nature as a father. Our conversation was brief and awkward, and he displayed the same behavior he had my entire life - disinterest.

After that phone call, I made the decision that if he would not try, I wouldn't either. I never ignored his phone calls because he would have to attempt to contact me in order for me to ignore them. Ultimately, my weak father chose his role in our family on the day I was born.

One day I received a message from my mother telling me that my father was dead, that he died a few months prior to her message. My late knowledge that my father died exemplifies our relationship and how insignificant we were to him. There was nothing in his will for us because that would take effort and care to do so. What I realized was that his death meant nothing to me because he was dead to me long before his corporeal death.

The legacy of the weak black father had to end, and it ended with me. Though being young and filled with worry about having a child in my early 20s, I never considered the life of fatherly weakness that my father exemplified. I grew into my adulthood and learned what true masculinity is. My son is my compass to keep me selfless in life.

My son doesn't know the pain of an effortless father, nor does he wonder if his father loves him. The weak black father has the responsibility to strengthen himself and take responsibility for his actions. The weak black father is not inherently weak. However, he has chosen to remain weak within the family structure, or has removed himself completely, fearing the hard work of fatherhood. I made the conscious decision to be the father that my father wasn't. Nobody should experience the emotional pain we suffered in a fatherless home. My son would definitely not know such pain.

What I am keenly aware of is the acceptance....no, the expectation.... that our black fathers will be broken, act broken, and never attempt to fix themselves. There is a median of low expectation for black men because of various factors which translate into low expectations for the black father.

The black father, like me, who is attentive to the needs, wants and desires of his children is applauded because he is not the majority. The broken black father wants acknowledgement and praise when he meets his paternal duties, and when there is no praise given, he will look for affirmation elsewhere.

The broken black father has no true expectation of himself to fight for involvement with his child. So, everyone else has given up on him as well. We cannot expect others to fight our battles in life. But the broken black father acts like the victim rather than acting as a man. A well-adjusted man stands up for what he believes, provides for the people he loves, and tends to his responsibilities regardless of his situation.

With the separation of the black father from the home, we perceive the black father's involvement as a charitable act rather than an obligation. As a community we have become familiar and friendly with the idea of the deadbeat black father because we have given up on the idea of a responsible, masculine, black father. Our black mothers then must harness the role of the masculine figure within the household, which discards the balance of the black family. The "man" who decides to neglect his family for his own selfish reasons, or lack of resoluteness, will be viewed as the American black cultural standard, so no one attempts to change this predicament. We shrug our shoulders and keep on moving.

We are not blind to what is going on, but we are sensitive about admitting our perception of the black father. The new black fathers look around them and they know that they are optional in existence, importance, and involvement. Decades ago, the black father who disappeared from the family might as well have disappeared from his community. Today, the black father who disappears from the family can live across the street. This man can live in personal comfort with his decision to extricate himself and repeat the process again with the next woman, if he chooses to. This man can continually call himself a man, in all his ignorance, while his child wonders when he will see him again.

The black community is now complacent in not criticizing this situation because we know far too many who grew up in this situation, and we don't criticize the norm much like we don't question a sunrise. The small ratio of black fathers who remain married to their child's mother, or at minimum remain very involved in the rearing of their children, is well-known to all in the black community.

Is it possible that we are too scared to point out the obvious because it will indict our own family in some way? People rarely take pleasure in highlighting dysfunction within their own family, so avoidance becomes our preferred method for emotional survival. When the black family avoids the topic of father dysfunction to avoid experiencing emotional pain, we are simultaneously avoiding the possibility of changing our community's perpetually self-inflicted pain. Every time we avoid this difficult discussion, we create another lost child in a world which requires direction.

MISSING FATHERS CREATE LOST CHILDREN

A real father helps to guide his children through childhood and prepares them for the adversity and virtue of adulthood. A father provides guidance to a seemingly lost child and instills confidence before the child starts to lack it. Missing that father figure results in children without direction and confidence. The father is the compass for the child's development and without the compass, many children are lost.

We have all seen lost children, but we just did not recognize that they were lost. The boy with irrational behavior in a daycare center. The hormonal, sexually driven teenage boy attempting to satisfy his urges with multiple partners. And the man holding his head low as he holds onto prison bars.

Boys who lack stability and direction look for guidance any place they can find it. If they are lucky, they'll find someone who is a positive influence. Far too often in the black community these lost boys find other lost boys in the form of gangs or look at terrible influences as examples of how a man is supposed to carry himself. Boys mimic male behavior like a mirror's reflection, and far too often the reflection is nothing to be proud of.

Though anecdotal, I have had many open conversations with men and women who have felt lost in life due to absentee fathers. The feeling of never belonging in the place you live, or not knowing the comfort of "home" are common. Even those who experience some accomplishments in life still have a sense of displacement. The feeling of being a lost child leaves you feeling unwanted, useless, or constantly questioning your worth. The saddest part about being a lost child is that you do not believe you will ever find where you belong in life.

My life struggles, in many ways, are due to my being a lost child. No powerful father figure ever presented himself during my childhood, nor did I have a positive male role model in my life to instill proper male behavior and virtues. This lost feeling compounded itself when I became homeless twice as a child.

During my childhood, I never truly felt comfortable with myself and I did not feel comfortable with where we lived. Before the age of 18, we lived in 4 states and multiple towns within those states. My feeling of being emotionally lost was also literal. When you move as much as I did, you do not know where your mental "home" is, nor where your geographic home is.

Like many adolescent boys, girls were of interest, but I had a level of desperation that only a lost boy can display. A lost boy like me only saw value in myself if a girl saw value in me. The constant rejection from girls made me constantly question my self-worth. Adolescence was an emotional rollercoaster for me. The endless rejection and reminders of belonging nowhere ate at me like a vulture on a rotting carcass.

The men you have witnessed who are incapable of keeping their urges in their pants are likely still the same lost boys looking for sexual acceptance. It is their only way of attempting to find the love they desire. These are also the same lost boys who create children like me - lost boys creating more lost boys. With a growing number of black boys being raised in single-parent households, the vision of manhood is shifting to the vision of the lost man. These lost men find lost women and create children who will subsequently struggle with finding acceptance in the world.

While the focus of my book tends to revolve around the black community, there is an epidemic of lost children in America in general. Being lost in society has nothing to do with race or culture. White males are responsible for the majority of mass school shootings, but they share something else in common, fatherless homes. The prison system is filled with lost black boys who were incarcerated after exhibiting reckless lost boy behavior. Our military is filled with lost boys looking for direction voluntarily and some experience, for the first time, a strong positive male role model while in the military.

Once you are a lost boy, it is extremely difficult to find your way, and it is even harder to shake that feeling. It does not matter how many years go by - it is a part of you. As an adult, I would move from apartment to apartment just about every year. I felt disconnected from where my home was. I would have fantasies about becoming a nomad because I thought maybe I am one of those people who is incapable of having an actual home. Even the idea of buying a house scares me to death. The concept of a foundational home that I have to stay in for an extended period of time brings chills down my spine. I have even questioned if America is where I am supposed to live in the long run. I have accepted that no matter how far I run in a particular direction, I will never outrun the sense of being lost.

Becoming a lost child is not asked for, it's placed upon you by your home circumstance. I would love to wake up one day and not have that sense of emptiness in my heart that was supposed to be filled by masculine fatherly love, but my father is dead now. My father's death represents the end of me asking for his love and now I must look within myself to love who I am. Like many lost children, we have an existential question to ask ourselves: "Do we become victims of our circumstances, or will we become victorious despite our shortcomings?"

Like many lost children, I spent decades feeling sorry for myself and wearing victimhood for societal warmth. Pity becomes the lost child's currency, and we can never collect enough of it. Outside acceptance is what drives us forward, but many of us never accept ourselves first. We are pathetic in our approach to making sound decisions, and when we don't create the life that we desire; we blame everyone else for our shortcomings. We cannot help what was done to us as a child, but we are responsible for our actions as an adult.

Though our fathers are supposed to be the architects of the compass within us, this does not mean that we are incapable of designing our own life compass as adults. We will struggle to find our way, but as long as we choose resilience over victimhood, we will consistently overcome. Many of us may need therapy to overcome the emotional pain or void within ourselves, and this is perfectly fine. Asking for help is not a weakness, pretending you are invincible is. I openly admit to seeing multiple therapists at different points in my life when I needed guidance, and I am only stronger because of it.

Too many lost black children believe they are unrepairable because they have been surrounded by people who find it useful to manipulate someone that is vulnerable. If they are not being manipulated, then they are being introduced to constant negativity that reaffirms the lack of a possibility of resurrecting their life situation.

If they believe that they will never amount to anything worth value, then they will live life as a valueless person. If they believe that their father's absence is due to the reaction to them personally rather than the weakness of their father, then they will carry the torch of victimhood as their only means of direction throughout their life.

The lost black boy is resentful, angry, pitiful, confused and disappointed. The lost black boy resents his father and once he grows old enough to resemble his broken father, he may repeat the behavior of his broken father. The lost black boy is angry because his broken father represents half of him - a half which is broken. The lost black boy is pitiful because he hopelessly wants his broken father to glue him back together so there can finally be an unbreakable bond between them.

The lost black boy is confused as to why his father does not try to change who he is for the sake of his offspring. The lost black boy is disappointed because of how inevitable it was that his broken black father made a choice a long time ago, and his choice was not his son. Once this cycle of emotion is completed for the lost black boy, if there is no interference, he will become who he always hated, the broken black father.

For the lost black girl, she missed out on a life of positive masculine love and male nurture that is irreplaceable. The father is the first and most important male influence for a girl, and if her father disappears, so does her positive male affirmation. The opportunity to see how a real man should treat a woman is what many of our black women have been missing since their childhood. The lost black girl never developed the ability to respect black male leadership within the home, so now she rejects it because it appears to challenge her existence.

When lost girls have no father, they will look for a new father. When lost girls have no foundational understanding of unconditional fatherly love, they will mistake sex for love and believe that love is conditional on their sexual promiscuity. Many of these lost girls have little self-worth and will use the power of female sexual desire to attract male attention once they are old enough to realize this phenomenon.

The culture of black female hypersexuality as seen in the lives of female musicians like Cardi B and television shows like Love & Hip Hop give them the understanding that their sexual worth determines their personal worth. This girl never questions the validity of this concept because on the surface it feels true. She is able to gain the male adoration that she never attained as a child with her father, and she views the quantity of male attention as being more important than the quality of male attention.

Every time the lost black girl looks at black culture for answers to her personal struggle, she is led down the path of destructive behavior that at minimum misrepresents who she is, who she is capable of becoming and what type of men she should value. When one parent is missing, someone or something will always fill in this gap, and popular black culture fills much of the lost black girl's emptiness with ignorance.

It is the ignorance of believing she is a surrogate for masculine energy rather than the embodiment of feminine beauty. Popular black culture instructs young black women throughout this country to act in a manner that repels masculine men and attracts feminized men who offer no future prospect for relationship or fatherhood. She is encouraged to outwardly express her emotional pain by being combative, manipulative and untrusting with men. Black culture never tells her to show restraint in her behavioral mannerisms, nor does it mind if she continually escalates it to a position of unattractiveness.

The lost black girl's downward spiral into hostility may also be accelerated because her missing father pushes her closer to mimicking her mother's behavior and even if it is negative and harmful, she may mindlessly repeat it despite the lack of positive results. When you hear of situations highlighting a teenage mother who was birthed by a teenage mother, it is an example of the legacy in which ruinous behavior is taught through daily experience. Due to a childhood of chaos, the lost girl will become more like her mother because consistency is what is most attractive to children. With a consistently missing father during childhood, she will expect men to be consistently missing in adulthood.

For the lost girls who don't become enamored with sexual currency, vulnerability becomes their greatest downfall. These are the girls who lack the experience of seeing proper male-to-female interactions. This fosters a greater possibility of being manipulated by men so that she behaves in a manner that reduces her self-esteem and makes her more easily controlled. She is caught in a quagmire when she combines her good intentions and poor male selections, thus creating a high likelihood of failing relationships, unhappiness and abuse. She is also blind when it comes to seeing common sense relationship red flags.

The lost boy and the lost girl grow up to be attracted to each other with a magnetism that ultimately ends up in chaos. Too many lost women believe that they can repair or give guidance to the lost man, when in reality her presence reduces his necessity to change, seek help or better himself.

She gives all her effort to push a man forward which causes her to slip backward in her personal progress. Her inevitable failure in this venture will present itself as a personal defeat, and will fill her head with questions of uncertainty about her worth as a woman based solely on the success of a man.

From the perspective of the lost black man, he grew up in an environment where women are placed on a higher pedestal the more masculine they are, and he tends to be attracted to this type of aggressive female behavior. If he grew up in a house filled with conflict, then he will gravitate towards women that clash with his potential growth into masculinity. When his partner reduces his manhood to maintain control in their relationship, it is the outcome that he expects because his mother acted in the same manner towards his father.

Manipulative women likely surrounded the lost boys who are dying for control. They have learned to utilize a variety of deceitful tactics because they feel powerless otherwise. Lying to themselves and others is a means of circumventing their feelings of inadequacy as a man. His false pride is manufactured to avoid others seeing who he truly is. He may exaggerate his self-worth, desirability, and finances so women will be impressed with his fictionalized character instead of his true unremarkable self.

There are essential masculine traits that many former lost boys are missing out on during our journey into manhood. Too many of us are afraid to be risk takers. We are agreeable to a fault, which makes it difficult for us to stick up for ourselves, even against people whom we love like our mothers. We have been conditioned to not trust our male instincts to take the lead in our relationships and careers, making us always second best to everyone else. This developmental handicap steers black men away from embracing healthy masculine traits that could help us excel in a multitude of ways.

Today, for many black men, our manhood has been mischaracterized, mishandled and demoted, and some of that blame has to go to the fathers who were too weak and too broken to sacrifice for their children. The fathers who dare to be selfish enough to choose abandonment are allowing their black boys to lose their voice because they aren't there to advocate for the male perspective within our community.

The disappearance of a male voice has created a streamlined negative reaction to black male concerns, perceptions, and criticisms. What's even worse is that when a man dares to raise legitimate concerns, a feminized former lost boy stands up to shut him down.

The cycle has to stop at some point. If you are a former lost boy, then it is up to you to become what your father wasn't. As a man nobody will hold your hand nor will they care about your emotional battles. Your childhood does not necessarily determine your life outcome. Family responsibility is not supposed to be your kryptonite that you avoid at all costs. Responsibility in caring for your family should be your priority and one of your greatest values.

Fatherhood is one of the most amazing privileges that a man can ever experience, and sacrificing for your offspring should be seen as honorable rather than being avoided at all costs. Learn from your struggle so that you are driven forward instead of backward for the sake of those who depend on something that is more valuable than anything that you could ever buy them - your love.

- CHAPTER 3 -

FEMINISM AND FATHERHOOD

"Once again, black women have to save black men..."

Thbis condescending quote was spoken by a black female friend years ago when we were discussing the topic of racism and my views on it as a black man. When she, a black woman, uttered these words to me over the phone, I was so stunned that she thought that this was perfectly acceptable to say to me as a black man. She audaciously believed that not only was it the black women's purpose to save black men but also delusionally believed that they had somehow saved us previously.

This unfortunately is a common view held by many black women who think they must save black men from ourselves because from her viewpoint we are incapable in many areas. As the conversation continued, she showed more ignorance by stating that black men are "only one step behind white people", meaning we have white sympathetic tendencies that are baked into our black male psyche.

This conversation is anecdotal of a greater problem that exists within the black community called the black female superiority complex. Obviously, this does not apply to all black women. However, the fact that this mindset exists demonstrates a disturbing plurality. This superiority complex displays a delusion of grandeur that purely because of our sex, black men are inept at being real men and that black women have to teach us how real men are supposed to behave.

These women have been given positive reinforcement whenever they acted with strong masculine behavior. Now they believe that their boundless aggressiveness is how men should be acting. They competitively measure their educational and financial success against men when in relationships rather than taking a partnership role. In the long run, their disdain for black men plays a part in why some of our black fathers aren't involved in the lives of our black children.

This superiority complex is upheld in all of black society. For example, it is seen in the trend of calling black women "Queens", "Bosses", "Divas" and saying that they possess a type of mysticism because they have "black girl magic". It is perfectly acceptable to slather black women with excessive praise even if in a particular situation it is unearned. When young black men get drafted into a professional league, they thank their mother unconditionally and even chuckle with the recognition that their first check has to go to buying their mom a house.

The greatest insult for a black child is when you insult his mother, not his father. The encouragement of saying our single-black mothers are the "Mother and the Father" and praising their mother on Father's Day only highlights the pedestalization of these types of women. There is no problem with showing appreciation for our black women and mothers when it's earned, but the problem is that for decades this praise has been coming at the expense of black men and fathers.

What I find interesting about my friend's complex about saving black men is that I know her past trauma of dealing with shit men and getting shit results due to it. The truth is that she wouldn't know how to attract a good black man that does not need saving, nor would she be attracted to him. The same black women who have delusions of grandeur choose terrible relationship partners as they are attracted to the very thing that they despise. The reality that they are attempting to create of the helpless black man is what they are truly attracted to for the sake of feeling superior within a relationship. Emotionally they feel the need to be in control because much of their life is out of control, hence the attraction to the lesser man that she can fix or save.

You can only feel superior to someone if you believe they are lower than you. Mainstream black media reinforces this mentality for the sake of pandering to a population of women for profit. Our community decades ago transformed into a strong matriarchy where the woman determines every aspect of her life, her family's life, and even whether a family is created. For various reasons, the black man is purely optional. The woman is viewed as a goddess compared to the peasant man. If she experiences failures, it's because of the man, but her success is because of herself.

For this type of woman, black men are merely accessories that accentuate who she is rather than being a bridge to potential happiness. At the worst end of this mentality, black men's usefulness is based on our ability to pleasure them whether it be through sexual pleasure or by what we can provide for them in the short term before our usefulness dries up.

Since black women can do everything that black men can, what is the use of black men? In this mentality, black men are purely redundant and not depended upon. A woman may have her own money, her own home, her own car, and now she can procreate without the stability of a relationship. To this particular type of woman, a relationship is transactional, and a man is disposed of as soon as she finds him to be a nuisance - or if he appears to alter the balance of control that she has within the relationship.

Once she disposes of her relationship with her baby's father, she knows that she can engage in a financial ménage à trois between her, her child's father, and the family court system. She knows that the family court system benefits her the majority of the time and that she can weaponize it to gain even more power over the man whom she now detests. She also understands that if she chooses to leverage her child's access to her father, she can get away with it because the man, in the eyes of the family court system, is guilty until proven innocent.

Although these are extreme situations, this is unfortunately the reality for many people. A life of being told that you are wonderful, perfect, and incapable of wrongdoing sadly coexists with doing everything possible to destroy your child's life prospects. There is a culture of openly talking about black fathers being deadbeats while denying the existence of immature and manipulative mothers. The cultural concept of black fathers being optional and undependable doesn't allow for many men to connect with their children.

This type of black woman who holds black men in such low regard will not trust him around her children as he is presumed to be naturally inadequate as a parent. This type of woman equates her poor relationship with her child's father with failure in the relationship between him and his children. The worst part is that this type of woman has wholeheartedly believed the lie that men do not care about their children's life outcome.

The irony of this type of strong independent narcissistic woman is not only that the men that she hates she is ultimately attracted to but also that if she births a boy she will attempt to raise him to be this same type of man. If she believes black men are weak, she will raise a weak boy. If she believes that the father's parenting style is too masculine, she will have no issue hindering his involvement. If she doesn't trust her child's father, she will also have trouble trusting her son. A house without a father alongside the mother, it is much like a country ruled by a dictatorship rather than a democracy. The mother is the supreme ruler regardless of her imperfections, and she has the backing of the black community to act in this manner.

Much of her behavior is a self-fulfilling prophecy when she creates conflict because she expects conflict or when she creates family separation because she expects family separation. She has no awareness of how masochistic she is when she creates a life of pain, dysfunction, and struggle due primarily to her poor decisions. When she chooses great sexual partners over great potential fathers, she's making a bed filled with nails for herself to sleep on. When she crushes the father's hopes of unification with his children, she's taking a jackhammer to her children's growth potential. The greatest privilege in America is not being white, it's having a healthy mother and father in the home.

This type of woman takes no responsibility for her part in the breakdown of the family because we have a culture of placating women by telling them they are perfection personified while their children suffer. We have a culture that laughingly degrades black men by dismissing them as trash and having miniscule expectations for them. Modern black culture has decided to adopt negative feminist rhetoric as the guide for how to treat black men. Feminism is without a doubt alive and well within black culture, and it has been for decades.

No one acknowledges that black men were forced to compete with the government as providers in their own home decades ago. No one acknowledges that feminist demands for stronger control over the family within the family court system gave little incentive for black women to keep black men around. No one acknowledges that the feminist movement fought for the legalizing of black genocide by abortion without the consent of black men. No one acknowledges the harm these actions have created because feminists have created a picture of men as the oppressor and cause of female suffering. All of this is part of an effort to destroy the black nuclear family. The goal has always been to divide the black family and conquer the children along the way.

Feminism as an ideology creates victims or harnesses those who feel victimized already. Feminism attempts to build up those victims by finding their male oppressor and giving them a narcissistic superiority complex along with it. Everything about this type of mindset is binary: good vs evil, oppressed vs oppressor, woman vs man. It is required that it be binary to draw a line in the sand as to which team you belong to, making it very simple for a woman to choose those who look like her even if it is self-destructive.

Female empowerment does not come without a casualty - male masculinity. Any ideology that cannot support itself without tearing down something else in the process is an ideology that is manipulative for the sake of gaining power. The feminist's constant focus on men is a distraction, and it leads women to not pay attention to the hypocrisy and flaws within their very own creeds. For example, feminism highlights masculinity as a negative but tells women to be more masculine to gain power. So, is masculinity good or bad? Feminists claim to care about families but spend most of their time fighting for the right to murder their unborn children. Feminists believe that it is bad when men sexualize women, but they encourage the average woman to be hypersexual and advocate for sex workers.

The popularization of hashtags like #MenAreTrash and #KillAllMen shows their complete disregard for the life of men. Imagine being a man going on social media to see someone as prominent as an editor of the Huffington Post, Emily McCombs, write the following: "New Year's resolution: 1. Cultivate female friendships 2. Band together to kill all men". This tweet is a perfect example of the open misandry that's acceptable to express regardless of its offensiveness.

Feminists cannot build themselves up unless they tear down men. When average people take notice of this type of hatred, publications that are sympathetic to their cause will easily cover for them. For example, The Atlantic published an article titled "A Twitter Hashtag Probably Doesn't Prove Feminists Want to Kill All Men". Oh, our mistake in interpreting this as a call to action. We know if this were #KillAllBlacks no one would say that this was a simple misinterpretation because it would be immediately shunned as it should be. However, feminism and the approval of said feminist ideology has infected our media, our government, the court system, higher education, and black America.

Feminist ideology has encouraged the burdensome lifestyle of being the "strong black woman", leading our black women down the path of most resistance. Black women across this country display their own "masculine" strength by putting themselves in positions of struggle, hoping they can overcome. Everyone is screaming for black women to travel down a bumpy road filled with self-inflicted drama for them to prove that they are capable and not dependent.

The people who are setting black women up for potential failure are doing so for their own personal gain. The black woman is told that she must be the superwoman savior for the black community, but with all the burdensome pressure she has to deal with daily, she can barely save herself.

As a product of a single-parent household, it is difficult for you to be shielded from the struggle that your mother endures. I felt at times that my mother's frustration with the situation of raising two children alone festered into a rageful reaction to get compliance from us. Watching my mother struggle at times to keep a roof over our head and give us the bare essentials with only one income made me sad even as a child.

No child wants to watch their mother barely keep their head above water. You're helpless to change the situation. One of the worst memories I have is watching my mother cry on the lawn of the apartment complex that we were being evicted from. My mother didn't cry often because she was thrust into the world of being the quintessential "strong black woman". So, you can imagine how traumatizing it was for me to witness my mother breakdown helplessly because we had no place to go.

Black women are focused on obtaining what they want, but often don't realize the uphill battle that they are bringing on themselves. The black woman who wants to feel ultimate liberation with her body and believes that she can have sex like a man since she can make money like one, in the long run will regret her faulty logic. People aren't willing to tell our young black women the genuine pain that is involved when it comes to being the sole provider for all financial, parental, and emotional needs of the family. The women who are going through this reality stay quiet because being strong and black means you cannot express your feelings of exhaustion for fear of appearing weak.

There are no hashtags for exhausted black single mothers, only hashtags for black female empowerment while secretly hoping you can muscle through one more dreadful day alone. Everyone stays silent on the feeling of loneliness that the so-called strong black woman has to experience to keep her status. Whether it is the loneliness of lacking companionship or of sharing parental support, these women are suffering with the sense of missing something important.

For black women across this country, this constant pressure leads to depression, insecurity, animosity, anger, and despair. Some of these women resent that they were not protected from experiencing this emotional pain by the father of their children. However, when she advocated for family dictatorship, she was unaware of the personal hurdles that she was putting in front of herself to obtain this illustrious female empowerment.

With great power comes great responsibility, however in the black community, our black matriarchs reject the responsibility to avoid any blame for some disastrous outcomes. It is understandable because we feel discomfort and shame when we are responsible for a negative outcome. It takes courage to raise your hand and be accountable for your faults in front of your community. However, if we teach black women (and women in general) that they are self-sufficient and don't need men, then there is no room for accountability and fixing what may be broken.

If there is a breakdown within a relationship, she takes zero responsibility for the separation of the father and the children. Even in a damaging situation where a woman committed adultery, it inevitably triggers a response asking what the man lacked for her to feel like she should cheat. If there is a situation where the mother chooses a man with zero life prospects or zero long-term investment, she accepts no responsibility for her part in the poor partner selection.

All in all, the strong black woman is a facade to hide the trauma that she is ashamed of. The strong black woman persona is extremely detrimental for women who have actually experienced trauma in their childhood, especially sexual trauma. She grows up resenting everyone who kept her from receiving the help that she needed. Because if she deviates from the strong persona, then it could put her blackness or womanhood into question.

The threat of being removed from either the black tribe or the woman tribe is enough to make a woman comply and continue to mask her internal trauma. This woman needs, not wants, to be called a "queen" because her personal value lies in how much affirmation she can receive. The opportunities for women to heal their brokenness will be slim if black culture doesn't allow for black women to be vulnerable. This type of woman is the broken girl who is all grown up but living a broken lifestyle and interacting with other broken people.

There is an underlying reason behind a woman who actively avoids being vulnerable with a man. It is because the pain and dysfunction she experienced as a child is sadly the pain and dysfunction that she is attracted to as an adult. Trauma is all she knows and sadly trauma is all she believes that she deserves. This is one of the many self-fulfilling prophecies that some black women end up experiencing.

The ploy of feminism is to harness black women's victimhood and community power to be the engine that helps push along the feminist narrative. On the flip side, black women use feminism to highlight their features while disregarding their faults, even if those faults may lead to their death. The fat acceptance movement is just another aspect of feminism which tells women that no matter their size, they are wonderful, gorgeous, beautiful and healthy.

Women are told they must be infallible, so they can't just be perfect mentally, they have to be perfect physically. We call black women "thick", "curvy" and "big boned" as they live their life suffering and dying from preventable health conditions. Feminists tell black women "Don't change who you are." but have no eulogy prepared when our black women lay dead in an extra-large casket.

Black women experience a higher rate of diabetes than any other demographic according to the US Department of Health and Human Services. Fifty-five percent of black women are obese, making them the most obese demographic in the United States according to the National Center for Health Statistics. The black woman's road has been paved with feminist good intentions, but it always leads to their demise when they become over-stressed, overwhelmed, overindulged and overweight.

Unfortunately, when many of our black women reach this devastating predicament, their sedation becomes validation by means of sex. No matter how many times women try to force feed themselves with other women's words of inspiration, it is not enough to fill what may be missing from her soul. Temporary pleasure is better than permanent misery, which is why sexual gratification is sought after so strongly. Imagine being overweight, stressed, depressed and alone. Why wouldn't someone's attention make you feel better? In her mind, the more attention, the better and society won't shame you for your sexual overindulgence; that would be slut shaming.

Feminism has removed the societal control we call "shame". No woman is allowed to feel bad for her actions because her actions are legitimate or not her fault. Have as much unprotected sex as you want because it decreases your loneliness. No shame in that. Eat as much as you want because emotional eating is emotional healing. No shame in that. Birth as many children with as many men as you want because you're the queen of your body. No shame in that. Kill as many unborn children as you want because you're just not ready to be accountable for your actions yet. No shame in that. When we shame nothing, we accept everything.

Living the life of "perfection" is living a life telling lies about yourself, which is what ultimately eats at the souls of these women. If they are lucky, they escape this trance-like state of thinking and graciously accept responsibility for their part of the downward spiral to move forward. The lucky ones are able to shape their womanhood how they want it to be and not how the feminist-ideologues deem it should be. The lucky ones embrace the beauty of femininity to attract healthy men instead of broken men. The lucky ones realize that they weren't only lying to their community, but they were lying to themselves.

The unlucky ones have shaped their existence around that cultural trope of black female strength so that it becomes cemented into reality. Her desire to fulfill this cultural ideal supersedes her desire not to suffer. Her hidden insecurity prevents her from questioning the narrative and challenging what is called normal. In some ways, she believes that because she already drank the poison, she must continue to pretend that it's medicine to save face. No shame, no accountability, no fault, and no regrets; drink up.

With all this internal and external conflict, she has forgotten that her children are like sponges to the energy that she projects. Her lost daughter models her insecurity after her mother's because she knows no differently. Our single mothers don't realize that they are their daughter's mirror and she is mirroring her mother's pain. A mother's actions will unknowingly duplicate themselves within her daughter's psyche, so that one day her daughter's strong black female persona will develop.

The older her son becomes, the more he will fulfill her desire for male companionship. His role as the son will overtime morph into the role of "son-husband". He is the "man of the house" and in this role he must fulfill her emotional needs by means of giving constant male encouragement.

When he inevitably fails at this role - which he didn't ask for - she will associate her son with all the other disappointing men that she once trusted. The difference is that her son is unable to escape her demands when the others could. The rollercoaster of disappointing his mother despite his efforts is one of many ways that his self-esteem gets destroyed. He will unfortunately associate his childhood failure to support his mother with a lifetime inadequacy to please women.

I know this feeling because that boy was me in some ways. I have powerful memories of trying to help my mother or fulfilling her household demands, but consistently falling short of her expectations. There were multiple times where I tried to do what she wanted, but it just wasn't good enough. She wanted me to do better in school, and I also fell short in that department. What made it worse was that after going to summer school two years in a row during high school, my mother stopped getting upset about my educational failures because she had come to expect little of me.

My disappointing results with my mother would translate into my various failing relationships, feeling inadequate as one relationship would fail into the next. When I would feel like I was trying my best to make a woman happy I was still failing. It would trigger a flashback to my childhood of not being a suitable boy. This gut-wrenching emotion of being a failure waiting to happen haunted me for decades and contributed to the destruction of many of my relationships. I had a fragile self-esteem sitting on the edge of a counter, waiting to hit the ground and break into pieces.

There was no father to catch me before I broke into pieces. When you only have one parent to impress, failure appears to be inevitable.

To summarize, feminism destroys the black family and prevents reunification. When people gravitate toward an ideology, they do so because it satisfies what is missing inside themselves. We tend to believe what we think is useful in moving us forward in our life. The problem comes when we believe untruths or when we extend our personal beliefs into ideologies that are hurtful to ourselves or others.

Feminism as an ideology is exclusionary in who it is meant to benefit and the term "benefit" may be a euphemism. Feminism uses terms like "strength" to get women to embark on behavior that is detrimental to their existence. They confuse women by having them believe that male nature is inherently bad, but to succeed you must act like a man.

Feminism is an ideology that wants all the power but none of the responsibility. Similarly, feminism wants women to be sexually promiscuous and without shame. Feminism claims to identify things that make women resent men, but all it does is manufacture what is not there. It is an ideology that supports female paranoia and encourages the hatred of men.

The major lie that feminists tell their new followers is that they are inherently victims and will always be victims. Most cults target people of a certain demographic to join their ranks as they are easier to manipulate. They purposely seek out people who have traumatic backgrounds like a broken home or abuse. These people don't need convincing that they are victims, they just need to know who the perpetrator is. Feminism allows victims to find their perpetrator and gives them the tool of ideological hatred to feed their victimhood.

The American black woman is the decision maker within the black community. Most black Americans grow up in a matriarchal world where the woman dictates our existence, and the male has little to no voice. While holding all the power in our community, black women are simultaneously told that they are victims of a variety of "isms". And once a victim, always a victim.

Many black women grew up in broken homes. No father was around to show them what masculine love looks like or to demonstrate healthy male to female relationships. Without this early male presence, they see any male attention as positive attention, even if it is from negative men. Once they develop a lifestyle of attracting undesirable black men, feminism will help guide them down the victim-path of casting aspersions on all black men, including their own missing father.

For years there has been a major push for feminists to embrace black women in particular because of the power they have been holding within the black household for decades. At the same time, black women have been looking for an ideological platform that excuses the negativity that they've grown up with and participate in. When a black woman is sexually promiscuous, it's for empowerment. When a black woman aborts her black child, it's her right. When she decides to birth the child of an undesirable man without the promise of a relationship, it's his fault. When she holds the burden of becoming the primary caregiver, it will be viewed as something that was inflicted upon her. At no point is the black woman at fault when feminism is the religion of choice. Words like "responsibility" will not be in her vocabulary.

Feminism does black women no favors. Nor does it empower them. Feminism harnesses their victimhood to another level, creating a dependency in which everyone else becomes responsible for their problems and faults. Feminism victimizes the black female by telling her that she will never improve her circumstance. So she must constantly embrace victimhood whenever she finds it useful.

Feminism encourages black women to exert false masculine energy and reject true femininity. She is encouraged to compete with any black man that she attempts to have a relationship with thus increasing the likelihood of family separation. The black father is a threat to the matriarchal dominant power structure of the modern black family, and feminists cannot have this power imbalance eliminated. The feminist view of the black father is that of a man who wants his power back. But the truth is that we want our family back.

Accusations of "victim blaming" are used to avoid any attempt at empowering someone. Not every person who claims to be a victim is one. Feminism requires victimhood to give its ideology legitimacy, and black women are the perfect target. Feminism is blocking black women from understanding their own power to change the state of black America instead of pointing their finger at someone else. Black women are being used for a greater political purpose - whether it be for votes or to help sway the opinions of a population of people - since black women are the ones that are in charge.

Black women are also being used for economic gain as there are whole industries that target black women for financial profit and manipulate them into keeping themselves separate from black men. For example, there are movies created that flaunt the strong single black woman who is over 40 who is "living her best life" and display the attractiveness of independence from men. When a black woman wonders why she is alone, there are books, seminars, and television shows that reinforce that there is nothing wrong with her and everything wrong with men because these industries need to keep the gravy train going.

The disappearance of fathers cannot solely be blamed on the father. Women are the gatekeepers to reproduction, so they have the responsibility to decide who they have sex with and who will father their offspring. It is the responsibility of black women to choose black men who are desirable for raising a family with instead of just their sexual pleasure. Far too often black women are playing Russian roulette with their body so they can have a few minutes of pleasure to hide their internal void.

Our behavior as a community is contributing to our own downfall and all we are doing is re-victimizing ourselves. The black women who are allowing broken black men to impregnate them are broken themselves. Many of these black women grew up in households without fathers and are confusing sexual attention with personal acceptance. Broken black men will give them momentary attention but permanent frustration will come with it. The black woman who grows up without her father tends to see men as optional and male involvement as a nuisance. Since a man did not serve any valid purpose during her childhood, she will see this as normal and have little to no desire to break this cycle.

These scenarios are common and can be clearly seen by any black woman who does not have feminism impeding her view. When a woman repeats the idea that black men are trash, she is doing the bidding of feminism. When she talks negatively about the type of men that she is currently sexually involved with, she will probably befriend feminism to help her manufacture a scapegoat for her own poor decisions. When she deflects all criticisms of her own actions towards men, she is acting as a feminist. When she downplays the importance of the black father, she creates more men like me who struggle to become emotionally secure throughout their lives.

The anger many black women experience stems from the disappointment they have with their own fathers who should have done more. I understand what it is like to miss out on the most important male influence in your life. But the problem is that many of the black mothers accept zero responsibility even though they often play a pivotal role in leading to the father's absence. This behavior of not accepting responsibility often gets passed down to their daughters who then repeat the cycle.

Criticisms are not given when the mother bad-mouths her child's father, refuses to allow her child's father access, manufactures lies about her child's father, and creates a narrative that paints the mother as a savior figure and the father as a devilish character. Feminists understand this complicated dynamic, and so they are ready to manipulate any black woman who is willing to listen. The result will be a passive disgust of black men and an expectation that they will be constantly disappointed by them.

The black woman has endured a lot throughout American history, but she did not do it alone. The black woman's pain has been felt by black men as well. The pain of not having fatherly love is a pain that black men are suffering from as well, but we are affected differently. Black women have allowed an ideology to keep us apart when we need each other the most.

Black men are not the enemy of black women, yet we are allowing a Marxist ideology to create a front-line offense within our own homes. Black male criticism of black women comes from a place of love, respect and concern, but we cannot keep pretending to not see the destruction of our families and the discouraging of male voices within our own community from speaking up.

Feminist criticism of male behavior is often based in hatred. Male criticism of female behavior is often for the purpose of relational peace. Fatherhood and feminism do not blend, and the more quickly we realize this, the more quickly our families will return to the mindset of victors instead of victims. If black women continue the anti-male rhetoric, our community will continue to sink into victimhood, which anchors us to the bottom of American society and prosperity. Hatred only breeds more hatred, and the black man you hate today will be the black boy that you are raising tomorrow.

– CHAPTER 4 –

AUTHORITY AND POLICING

"The dominant role of fathers in preventing delinquency is well-established. Over forty years ago, this phenomenon was highlighted in the classic studies of the causes of delinquency by Sheldon and Eleanor Glueck of Harvard University. They described in academic terms what many children hear their mothers so often say: 'Wait till your father gets home!' In a well-functioning family, the very presence of the father embodies authority, an authority conveyed through his daily involvement in family life. This paternal authority is critical to the prevention of psychopathology and delinquency."

—The Heritage Foundation

"The Real Root Cause of Violent Crime:
The Breakdown of Marriage, Family and Community"

Leftist elites love to point to poverty as the major reason why there is an exorbitant amount of black criminality and degeneracy. But black Americans aren't the only group of Americans who have experienced poverty. Although about 21% of black Americans live in poverty (2019 - Kaiser Family Foundation), 17% of Hispanics and for comparison's sake, 9% of whites live in poverty as well.

"Blacks are incarcerated at a high rate due to a history of slavery." If this were true, then we could look at our incarceration rates in the early 1900s and see a similarity between the two. Yet during this earlier period black imprisonment was more proportionate to the population size. In 1930, 65 years after the abolition of slavery, a time when Jim Crow laws were fully in effect and the KKK was not only running rampant on the streets but was also in public office, 22% of the state and federal prison population were black and 78% were white. During this decade blacks made up almost 11 % of the population. Forty years later in 1970, post-Jim Crow, it rose to 39% black imprisonment despite the fact that blacks were still 11% of the population.

Ironically, the freer we've become, the more we've imprisoned ourselves. So how does this happen? If we listen to black intellectuals, the media and the social justice narrative, it is due to racism. But if that were true, how do you explain less imprisonment during a time of legalized oppression in half of the country? Does racism put a gun in a black person's hand and cause them to pull the trigger? Does racism force black people to sell drugs to their own community? leftist ideology wants us to believe that black people have no control over their destiny and that any excuse, no matter how unprovable it is, should be a legitimate cause for horrible behavior.

Poverty is not the root cause of our issues; it is the end result. Racism doesn't even make the top 10 list of issues that black people experience daily as a life hindrance. Both are a distraction from finding the actual source of the issues within our community. And by not identifying the true source of our problems, we will continue to be in the same position year after year, decade after decade. If we want true solutions, we have to stop entertaining simplistic fallacies that put the blame on everyone else so that we can lazily avoid looking at ourselves.

The black single-parent household makes up 70% of black households and it is growing. These homes are primarily single black mother dominated households. The dominance of women in black America and the absence of black fathers in the homes, especially for young black males, is the ultimate source of our issues.

If we look at crime statistics, it is overwhelmingly obvious how disproportionately crime is committed by black males. But we have the cause and effect all wrong. Crime is related to a child's family connection and especially for boys, a connection to their first and most important male figure in their life, their fathers. Without this connection, lost boys are created, and they will be eaten up by any malignant force that resides within black communities.

From a psychological viewpoint, the healthy father represents a child's first authority figure. Traditionally, the mother represents the role of a nurturer in the family, while the father is supposed to be the authority figure who helps to disseminate fair judgements within the family unit. This does not mean that the parties are incapable of switching roles occasionally. But women sometimes have trouble going against their instincts as nurturers to discipline in a measured way.

Both authority and nurture are necessary, and they are equally important. Too much authority will be harsh. However, too much nurturing is detrimental as well. Both authority and nurture are needed for a healthy and well-adjusted child to feel balanced in an unforgiving world. If you grow up without proper authority, you will be in a constant clash within our society. If you grow up without proper nurturing, you will not be balanced in how you interact with people, nor will you care about the feelings of others.

The absence of authority and the absence of respect go hand in hand. The child who doesn't respect authority will not respect teachers, officers, judges, and even their bosses later in life. They will be in constant conflict with people in authority because they have been in a position of self-authority for the majority of their life. Young men with overbearing single mothers can lose respect for this authority once they are bigger than their mothers and can withstand physical punishment. For many single black mothers, physical punishment is their only solution for adjusting black male behavior. But as stated before, authority without measurement appears harsh.

Many mothers find it difficult acting as the measured parental authority figure and when they are thrust into the world of single motherhood, they may use physical punishment as their only means of behavioral adjustment. But physical punishment without measurement yields temporary results for young men. Injuring a child to the point of crying does not create respect. It creates fear and resentment.

A healthy father understands this and may never find the need to put his hands on his child because he understands how to exert authority in healthier ways that yield long-lasting results. Also, healthy fathers understand the desire of young boys to gain approval from their father, so fatherly disappointment can be enough to adjust a boy's behavior.

Fathers see themselves in their sons, and sons see themselves in their fathers. This path of passed down masculinity is mostly lost within the black community. The missing masculine authority figure for young black males is contributing to the downfall of black men and failing to recognize this only perpetuates our shortcomings and suffering.

As obvious as I am making this sound now, it took me decades to fully recognize the impact of missing a father in the home and even more so, a healthy father figure. There is a quote I heard once that seems fitting. "A two-parent household is a democracy, a single-parent household is a dictatorship". There was no counterbalance when it came to our home, and no matter how unfair I thought something was, I had no one to counter potential unfairness within the home.

In a single parent home, there is a clear lack of balance when it comes to discipline, because single mothers lack the time and patience to cope well with discipline problems. They are shouldering the load of two and will constantly aim for the quickest solution. But short-term gains with discipline yield long-term losses. The more the child acts out, the more the mother resorts to physical punishment and the less effective it becomes. It takes time and patience to understand why a child is acting in a certain manner. But the nature of being a single mother makes this extremely difficult, on top of the fact that they are not naturally disciplinarians.

My personal relationship with my mother was sometimes tumultuous. As a boy without a father and moving from town to town and state to state, all I had was my mother and my sister. As my sister got older, she distanced herself from me and at times resented me because my mother made her responsible for me at a young age since she was older. My mother's situation forced a child to become my part-time guardian, and this resulted in my sister not having a typically fulfilling childhood like she should have had. In my sister's child-brain, me being born, was the reason for this extra pressure that was placed upon her due to not having a second parent in the household.

It's not unusual to give children extra responsibility, however it is unfair to place a child in the position of becoming another child's caretaker for hours on end on a near daily basis. Nor is it fair to place the responsibility of discipline on an older child for a younger child's behavior. This was the reality for my sister's and my relationship for years. Not only was authority badly handled in our family, but it was also sometimes placed into the hands of a child who should not have been burdened with that responsibility and did not know how to discipline well.

When my mother was home, her patience for typical child behavior was at times thin. A hint of disobedience or not following given directions would cause hysterical yelling or at worse a beating. When you are in this type of environment, your behavior isn't based on respect for your parent as an authority figure and wanting to please them. Your behavior is dictated by the fear of potential repercussions because they are harsh and volatile.

What's even worse is that culturally, we've normalized corporal punishment and blur the lines between discipline and abuse. We now have grown black men and women who continuously applaud their single mothers for senselessly beating them as if there were no other way to be handled as a child. Many of us behave like we are experiencing Stockholm syndrome when we thank our abusers for unleashing their fury upon our flesh.

The response from my mother was sometimes unpredictable. When you are a child who can't predict what is going to happen, you build anxiety around every potential situation that could get you in trouble. This anxiety carried over into most of my interactions with people throughout my life as social anxiety.

I want to make something abundantly clear; I don't see my mother as physically abusive. At times she used emotionally manipulative tactics. My mother's situation as a single mother made it easier for her negative discipline techniques to flourish, even if she had the best of intentions. As difficult as it is at times to get along with my mother, I still love her. I understand her past and the psychology behind her behavior, although I do not excuse it. We cannot help what happens to us as children, but we are responsible for correcting our behavior as adults.

"In 1968, 94% of American adults approved of spanking a child, but by 2012, the figure dropped to 70%. While most of American parents still approve in the spanking of children, some are more likely to spank than others. According to a recent study of 20,000 kindergartners and their parents, black parents are the most likely to spank their children (89%) and Asian parents, least likely (73%). White and Hispanic parents fell in between, at 79% and 80%, respectively."—The Society Pages "Race, Spanking and Shame: Dimensions of Corporal Punishment" / Data taken from General Social Survey (GSS)

The parental discipline I faced was not authority based on respect, it was forced authority. You may have heard people state that they "demand respect" but respect can't be commanded, it is earned. Respect is mutual and understood by both parties. Without this respect, authority is based on fear. The fear of a child who complies with their parent's demands solely, so they aren't assaulted by someone that they love is emotionally abusive. No one wins in this formula and everyone gets hurt. The mother's frustration with her child's disobedience will be overwhelming for her and tiresome. The child's frustration with constantly wondering when the next emotional explosion is going to occur will disable him with anxiety. This cycle revolves around the most obvious missing factor, the father.

I am reminded of a time when I was walking down a street in my hometown when I saw a woman and her small child walking quickly while she forcefully held his hand. This boy couldn't have been older than 2 years old based on his size and his ability to walk. The mother was constantly yanking on his arm and grumbling "Hurry Up!" and complaining to him that he "always does this". Keep in mind, this boy wasn't crying, yelling or misbehaving at that moment in any fashion. This action of violently yanking her child's arm was the outward manifestation of her frustration with her situation and not her son. But he will probably be the figurative punching bag for all her problems. She was a black mother and statistically, she's likely a single mother.

There is an acceptance within black culture of a lack of respect for male authority. Every problem has its source and before a child is created, the woman plays a role in choosing who she has sex with that might lead to her pregnancy. Women are the gatekeepers of life, and they are the last defense to weed out the weak and undesirable men in our population. This does not mean that men hold no responsibility, however the modern woman has many forms of contraception to prevent pregnancy and unfortunately has the right to singularly decide to abort an unwanted child. With this as the reality, women have the power and authority to choose when they have a child and with whom.

The sexual revolution within the black community has resulted in black women choosing pleasure over responsibility. There are many black women who are choosing undesirable black men for reckless sexual pleasure that is resulting in a family unit that is unlikely to be successful. These women do not look for potential fathers nor men that they truly respect. On the contrary, they are choosing men based on animal-like instincts of outward appearance and sexual attraction. This leftist view of sex has also infected the minds of our black girls, contributing to the high levels of teenage black pregnancy, which is double that of white teenagers (27.5 per 1,000 black females aged 15-19 compared to 13.2 per 1,000 white females according to the CDC in 2017).

When these women become impregnated by the "undesirables", they will see the bottom of the barrel black male as representative of all black men. If their baby's father is disinterested or broke, then all black men must be this way. There is something severely wrong when a woman allows a man to enter inside her, even when she does not respect him. The black women who subscribe to this mindset disregard the importance of black male authority in their children's development.

It is no surprise that your odds of being a single parent increase tremendously if you are a product of a single-parent household. Children repeat the behavior of their surroundings, even if the behavior is detrimental to their existence. If you're a child of a single parent, you will probably see this as normal and acceptable, so you will not proceed with caution when you venture into sexual activity.

Similarly, having parents who are homeowners makes you more likely to want to own a home and succeed at doing so. If your parents are abusive, you are more likely to enter a relationship where you will be abused or where you will be the abuser. If your family is broken and does not receive intervention, you will probably create a broken family. Without the black father, the black family is undoubtedly broken.

I know this tendency to repeat what we see in our childhood because my initial disciplinary style as a father mirrored how my mother disciplined us. My mother spanked us, and so I occasionally spanked my son when he was very young. My mother was easily frustrated, and I was like this at times with my son. At the time, I did not have a psychological understanding as to why I was behaving in such a way that even then I didn't like. Behaving in a manner that we dislike as a parent often results from unconsciously modeling behavior from someone who was influential in our childhood.

We are influenced by our environment and the only way we can alter this behavior is by acknowledging that there is a problem. All human behavior is capable of being changed, but acknowledgement of a problem must come first to change habitual behavior.

There came a point early in my son's life when I realized I did not like spanking my son and that I was at times unnecessarily impatient with him. My son wasn't some sort of special case or even necessarily bad at a young age. He was your average child behaviorally, so my approach was not proportionate to the situations that were presented. I realized that I was being instinctually reactive instead of being thoughtfully measured. I saw that my behavior was not that of a thinking person but of an emotional person and they are mutually exclusive.

When you are emotional, you are not thinking clearly, however when you are thinking clearly, you can consider not only your own emotional response but also the emotional responses of others. The more I practiced thinking before responding to my son in situations requiring discipline, the more I was able to be balanced in how we interacted. I was able to discuss with him the nature of his actions. I was no longer angry or desperate for his compliance because we developed a mutual understanding. Our relationship is now one of love and respect, in other words of healthy authority.

My initial method of disciplining was not my own. It was my mother's. My mother didn't have to tell me how to display authority over my son. She modeled it when I was a child and without realizing it, I repeated this behavior with my son despite not liking how it made me feel when I was a child. My decision to change was rooted in me not feeling good about how I was handling these situations and how it felt unnatural for my responses to be so disproportionately aggressive.

The reason it felt unnatural was because I was modeling the behavior of a single mother who had utilized feminized aggression to exert control over my child. Without a healthy father in my life, I lacked the ability to develop healthy masculine ways to earn respect as an authority figure instead of using force. When men attempt to use feminine tactics, it results in men that are off balance in a variety of ways. And the same can be said for women who attempt to be masculine. The black single mother is viewed as a powerful authority figure. But the type of authority figure they become is what ultimately matters.

After this personal awakening, my relationship with my son improved for the better. I cannot remember the last time I put my hands on him because it is truly unnecessary to even do so. Every adult that encounters him comments about how well behaved he is, how pleasant he is to talk to and how calm he is. I cannot take all the credit for his development because his mother exemplified the balanced feminine energy that he needed in his life, so he can also be a caring human being. Children need both masculine and feminine influence to have a balanced outlook on life. But we are encouraging off balanced parenting which is detrimental to the well-being of black children across America.

The modern black family is hardly a family, nor does it have a healthy structure. Men have been viewed as the authority figures for the family; not so they can callously hold control but so they can be sacrificially responsible for the safety and well-being of their family. The role of the black father is meant to ensure that his entire family could survive anything that was put in front of them. Feminist ideology tells us that men having family authority is a power grab. But those who say this ignore the responsibility that must come along with authority. The modern single black mother, knowingly or not, follows the feminist doctrine to a T and yields fear-based authority with the backing of family courts.

With missing fathers and anger towards men as "trash" or "dogs", how do we think these women will see their own sons? My mother never married and barely had any relationships with any men throughout my entire life. A few years ago, I curiously asked her, "How come you never got married?" at which she replied, "Because all men cheat". I'm not trying to pick on my mother, I'm only trying to demonstrate that her way of thinking isn't uncommon. If women really feel that all men are one step above scum, how do we think they will treat their boys who will grow up to become men? Even when I asked her that question, she couldn't see the irony in giving that answer to her son, a grown man.

Are we to believe that this anti-male rhetoric completely disappears once it involves their own male offspring? Are we to believe that when this boy grows up to look like the man that she despises, she will be able to treat him differently than his father? Should we expect that somehow, she will be able to have a positive relationship with her own black male child?

The phrase "You're just like your father" in the black community is a pejorative, not a compliment. It simply means that the boy is in the beginning phase of disgusting his mother, much like how his father does. This matters in the equation of respect for authority, because if the authority figure doesn't respect those whom they are in control of, the subordinates will not respect them back.

If the black mother sees her black boy as an inconvenience, much like the black mother from my hometown stated regarding her son that he was "always doing this" meaning "always inconveniencing her", then eventually respect is not given back. Children are inexperienced, not stupid. They know when they are blamed for something that they did not do and are looked down upon unfairly. Words carry meaning and when a black woman talks negatively about black men, it will inevitably alter the perception she has of her male child… as well as the child's perception of himself.

"Girls whose fathers left either before they were born or up to age 5 were seven to eight times more at risk of becoming pregnant as an adolescent than girls living with their fathers. A father's departure between ages 6 to13 suggested a two to three times greater

69

risk of becoming pregnant."—Psychology Today "Absentee Fathers and Teen Pregnancy"

Daughters of single black mothers are likely to carry the legacy of modeled illegitimacy into their adult life. The life of a singular female authoritarian will not appear unusual for these future black mothers, and they will proceed with their sexual exploration haphazardly. They've been told that men, especially black men, are simply optional pieces to the puzzle and that including a black man will result in reducing her authority within the family. She will be raised to not look for love and care through family togetherness, but instead for power through independence.

To a girl who is being raised to be a future authoritarian, power limitations are extremely unappealing. The black female's view of family life in which she would need to share authority with a man while also compromising with him will not be at all appealing to her.

These girls are not only missing their fathers, but they are also missing seeing the importance of male authority for the health of their child. The young black women who have experienced this loss will transfer their frustration and lack of expectations to the next man who resembles her own uninvolved father. When she chooses to yell at men instead of reasoning with them it is because she was never able to express her frustration to her missing father. Her guard is up because she doesn't want to be that hurt little girl anymore, and her need to take control is because her home life was out of control from an early age. As an adult, she will now push people away before they can get close enough to disappoint her as her father did.

What these young black women don't understand is that pain can be transferred and that we are constantly learning behavior from people who are significant in our lives. We model behavior whether it is positive or negative and for these young black women, they are learning the lifestyle of sole familial responsibility, parental burden, and unsuccessful relationships. There is also constant excuse making so black women don't have their feelings hurt when they mindlessly engage in the very behaviors that trap them in failure and poverty.

The strong black woman profile that we hold in such esteem is often riddled with emotional pain and delusions of superiority because as a community we have accepted matriarchal toxicity to avoid conflict. The black family was never patriarchal because both men and women had their roles that were extremely important to the survival of the black family. The black father was the leading authority figure, but he was not singular in all decision making. The modern black female believes that her relationship with potential black fathers is purely transactional and inevitably temporary. With the family authority figure gone, our young black women learn to keep black men at constant arm's length and our young black men learn to not respect authority figures, even if their life depends on it.

Many young black men who have lived a life with only feminine authority figures feel threatened when faced with masculine authority. These black men are highly emotional, sensitive, and much like their single mothers, see male authority as a threat. Some of these men have lived a life that lacked any positive male role models to show them how to respect discipline. They have led a life of bending the knee to the woman of the house, so that the thought of bending the knee to a man in authority is seen as just another way of being kept down.

Even for me, there was always an intimidation factor when it came to male authority, since it was a rarity. Masculinity felt threatening because I had been indoctrinated my entire life to place female authority on a pedestal. Although my mother attempted to have me participate in sports so that I would be around other men, the couple of hours away with the guys was no match for the constant feminine interactions at home.

The lack of respect for male authority along with their own personal insecurities about what manhood comprises is killing black America's potential and sometimes killing black people. The fear of female rejection if one disobeys is limited in its success. The methods of guilt, de-masculinization and physicality to keep the black boy in line will only produce fearful black men who associate pain with love and female relationships. Thus, they choose sexual stimulation outside of the home instead of seeking family stimulation because it often involves getting hurt. Mainstream black culture reinforces this dysfunctional family structure and sees it as a natural part of being black so that it is viewed as normal and unchangeable.

These mentally victimized black men will enter the world not caring about what other men think of their behavior. The reality is that the black boy without a father grew up to not respect other men in general and likely grew up not respecting themselves. A man that doesn't respect himself is among the most dangerous beings in the world because his natural aggression is without bounds. When these men encounter authority figures, they will respect them as much as they respect their own fathers. And if their father was not present, their respect wouldn't be either.

"A very real connection between delinquent behavior, and single-parent families, in particular mother-only families, produces more delinquent children than two-parent families. The absence of fathers from children's lives is one of the most important causes related to children's well-being such as increasing rates of juvenile crime, depression and eating disorders, teen suicide, and abuse."—International Journal of Science and Research (IJSR) "Effect of Single Parent Family on Child Delinquency" (2012)

The mind of a criminal is one that does not respect authority, property or personhood and does not have boundaries that they aren't willing to cross. The dis-proportionality of the American criminal system being full of black bodies has less to do with race and more to do with early family structure and cultural standards. The financial component is not even the biggest determination because finances don't shape one's moral conduct, they only allow one to avoid certain life roadblocks.

Poverty is used as a crutch in the black community, but crutches are meant to be temporary, and our excuse of poverty seems to be permanent. How do we explain the many black people that were poor decades ago that did not end up in prison? How about the poor people of today that have avoided prison? Were they lucky or did they exercise decision making that avoided incarceration as an option?

For some young black men law enforcement is the antithesis of what they are familiar with and what they have learned to respect. Law enforcement is overwhelmingly male and when our black boys encounter police, they show little respect for male commands even if it puts their own life at risk.

Black boys can be combative when it comes to obeying simple instructions and they see law enforcement as masculine oppression, holding a similar mindset as their black mothers. They think that no man is going to tell them what they can and cannot do. Resisting arrest becomes automatic when this is one's mindset. It does not occur to them that this escalation in an interaction with a police officer may lead to their own death.

They view authority figures as animals, hence the usage of a term like "pig" to describe law enforcement. When a black male who has this mindset struggles with police, they do not see themselves as a potential threat to the officers because they do not take responsibility for the danger they put others in. They are not familiar with the concept of caring about the life of someone whom they are not in a relationship with. They cannot see themselves as someone who is dangerous to their own community. So, they will fight all attempts to bring punishment for their behavior at the hands of male authority. If these young black men are killed because of their noncompliance, their single black mothers will be sure to blame the male authority figure as we see all the time.

When we are too scared to criticize each other, hold each other accountable and socially police our own community, we become the American pariahs that perpetuate a cycle of misbehavior, lawlessness and victimhood. We have allowed the new leaders of the black community to be primarily women. But leadership typically comes with criticism and responsibility at which these black female leaders balk.

The black men of America are encouraged to take a step back and let the women suffer while attempting to carry the full responsibility of parenthood. The black men who choose to uphold their obligation of fatherhood understand their importance of demonstrating measured authority for their children and they know that their presence can help to save their son's lives. The young black men who are dying on the streets due to gang violence are lost boys who are attempting to find their importance within a culture that celebrates blocking the one man who is meant to build their self-esteem: their father.

– CHAPTER 5 –

POISONOUS BLACK IDEOLOGY

January 15th, 2019 – David Webb, a conservative radio host on Sirius XM radio, had a long phone conversation live on his radio show with his guest Areva Martin, a prominent political commentator and CNN analyst. Their conversation was coming to an end and David dared to utter the sentence, "I never considered my color the issue. I considered my qualifications the issue." This sentence triggered the leftist reactionary statement, "Well, David, that's a whole other long conversation about white privilege and the things that you have the privilege of doing that people of color don't have." David was perplexed by this statement. He replied, "How do I have the privilege of white privilege?" Areva answered by stating "By virtue of being a white male you have white privilege. It's a whole long conversation that I don't have time to get into."

Areva made a vital mistake in her assumptions. David's response said it all: "Areva, I hate to break it to you, but you should've been better prepped. I'm black."

WHAT DOES IT MEAN TO BE BLACK?

Is it how you dress? Is it how you carry yourself? Are all black people supposed to be the same? There are an endless number of questions I have asked myself over the years to figure out what it means to be black.

First, we must establish that blackness is used to measure someone's compliance with the mainstream black cultural narrative and what is viewed as acceptable black behavior. If you willingly deviate or criticize aspects of black culture, your allegiance comes into question as if you are a traitor. In many ways, modern black culture has cult-like tendencies. Defectors of the black ideology are demonized and described as either wanting to be or acting "white". If you disagree with what the congregation decides to advocate for or protest against, you will not be allowed in the church with good graces.

Within a religion, you can choose what part of the gospel you feel makes sense to you without harsh criticisms from others. In most religions, you're allowed to personally interpret doctrine with the understanding that we all see things slightly differently. Black ideology is less like a religion and more like a cult due to this rigidity of thought and unacceptance of interpreting what it means to be black on an individual level.

Cults typically have a charismatic leader type who pretends to lead for the sake of the greater good, but often it's for their personal benefit. The black community utilizes charismatic ministers and pastors who speak with a particular vocal cadence as our cult-like leadership. When they say "Jump", we say, "How High?" and when they say, "No Justice", we instinctively reply with "No Peace".

In America, there is no other racial demographic that is expected to have a leader of a community that includes millions of people - except for black people. There may be advocacy groups for other ethnic groups, but no one expects them to be the thought leaders for an entire population. To be black in America means that you must suspend all personal beliefs publicly to show unity with people who share your pigmentation. I'm not

76

disillusioned enough to believe that all black people actually believe every single narrative, but stating their disagreement with a particular narrative publicly risks excommunication from the tribe. We are expected to always show unity verbally, even if internally we question the beliefs and motives of our "leaders".

Black Americans are quick to deflect any criticisms that are directed at the ideology, even if they are legitimate. If we feel that someone outside our race is attempting to tear us down, that is inexcusable. But we tear at each other all the time. Where is our unity when we murder each other at higher rates than other races? Where is our unity when we unapologetically disparage black men? Where is our unity when we call each other niggers during a confrontation? Our unity is our public persona for people outside the community, to protect us from being seen for what we really are - flawed.

No community is perfect, but black ideology states that we must repeat self-help lines like "black is beautiful" while we act ugly. We embrace dysfunction and excuse chaos as long as it's committed by another melanated soul. If someone within our cult commits a crime, it must be because of outside influences, because blackness must be perfection.

To be black in America, you must romanticize struggle, whether it's present day or historical. We must reminisce about a time of Civil Rights marches and use our imaginations to feel the anguish of slavery. Why do we torment ourselves with these thoughts from a time long ago? We must always find a way to equate present day wrongs to the past to legitimize our disdain for America. When we speak of American black history, it must only be from the perspective of the victim, skipping over the multitude of examples when we were victors.

To be black in America, you must be okay with hypocrisy as long as it benefits you. We can complain all day, every day about people prejudging us because of our pigmentation, but it's perfectly fine if we label all white people as thinking the same, acting the same way and wanting the same things. We are able to vocalize critical thoughts about other demographics publicly, but our flaws are not meant to be spoken about outside of the group. If someone outside of the cult attempts to call you out on your racism, simply change the definition of racism by adding caveats like "power plus privilege". Sadly though, this means that even black people believe that we are incapable of obtaining power or privilege.

To be black in America, you must always have low expectations of your fellow black cult members. The black expectation for success is always set at a minimum, so when we overcome, it is an even greater feat. We treat black upward mobility like a glitch in the matrix rather than an outcome of hard work and perseverance. In some cases, we believe people are just lucky to escape poverty or that it was simply given to them because for the past few decades in many black households, handout culture has been normalized. Since we believe that we are helpless victims to an unjust system, then the only way for us to survive is by the good graces of this unjust system. We believe we are owed something just for existing or for the pain inflicted on people before us. We don't understand that no one will be a bigger advocate for yourself than you.

The cult of blackness that acts as if it cares about black people has false leaders, excuse making tendencies, low expectations of its black congregation, and gives all power to their perceived devil - white people. Ironically, the black ideology is extremely white centric and believes that only they can save black people because they have all the power. The black ideology sees our situation as the unfortunate byproduct of the existence of the counter ideology called "whiteness".

"Whiteness" has all the power, all the responsibility, all the accountability, all the hubris, all the desires and all the adulation. What is left if whiteness has swallowed all the positives? Obviously, the negatives. Blackness finds pride in all the negative attributes because at least we can call this our own. When we are called out on this, we will point the finger at our white counterparts as the thieves to our possible perseverance, of course. If white people have all the power, then we have none of the responsibility. The mindset of the victim is to expect to be victimized and to creates scenarios for their victimization. The creation of a white monster and waiting to be saved is our modern-day routine to remain the victims in American society.

To be black in America means that you are black first, everything else second. For many people, their religion defines who they are morally and how they approach life. Black-dogma works in a similar way. You are black first in all aspects of your life, in success or failure. If you achieve your goals, it's due to the strength of blackness. If you fail, it's due to someone else preventing your success due to you being black. If anyone takes notice of this constant need to mention our pigmentation, then they are the ignorant ones, not us. Our ideology says that everything is about race and nothing about our actions. Since we operate as identitarians, we believe that everyone else proceeds with a similar mindset, increasing the possibility of us manufacturing racial conflict from any ambiguous situation.

If you're a student who fails a class, it must be due to your teacher's animosity towards your black skin rather than your shortcomings as a student. If you don't land the job that you wanted, it couldn't be due to your lack of qualifications or how you presented yourself during the interview. It must be due to the company's racism. If a store clerk is disrespectful towards you, it couldn't be that they are terrible to everyone they encounter or that they are having a bad day. It must be that they live their life waiting for the moment when they can direct their aggression at the next black person they encounter.

Since the black "congregation" sees their race as the most important aspect of their life, they believe that it is the same for everyone else, which is undoubtedly false. The over emphasis on race is the byproduct of listening to racial rhetoric throughout the lifespan of the average black person; believing that something that they were born with and unable to control is ultimately who they are. The thought process is the following: If I see myself as black first on the scale of life importance, then you must see yourself as white first so that when you see black skin you must be treating me accordingly.

Much of mainstream black ideology incorporates the practice of psychological projection. You may have seen situations where a spouse claims that their significant other is indulging in adultery, but you later find out that the accuser is the one who is committing adultery in the relationship; this is projection. Modern black ideology teaches black Americans to project onto others what we are actually doing.

For example, we project our reactionary claims of racism onto others because we are often racist towards non-blacks. We project that whites are willfully violent towards blacks because we are willfully violent towards other blacks. We project that white people want to be treated with special privileges because we are dying to be treated with special privileges. We claim that everyone "steals" from black culture because we "steal" from other cultures all the time. Worst of all, we project when we claim that no one believes black lives matter because we don't even believe all black lives matter.

Cult members take advantage of emotion because emotion always overshadows logic. When their charismatic leader tells them the impossible, it takes blind emotional faith to move forward with his commands. The cult of black ideology has similar tactics that focus on emotion over logic, feelings over statistics, and reaction over patience. Our emotions lead us to follow false prophets, vote for political panderers, and cry for criminals. These are the individuals that profit off our pain and make sure to never allow you to move forward. A singular anecdotal incidence transforms into actual evidence of a systemic problem. The real forbidden n-word in this cult is not nigger, it's nuance.

Only the dissidents of black culture attempt to use nuance, which only increases the number of smears launched in their direction. The dissidents of the cult are not only excommunicated, but they are also actively demonized by other black people with the same racial slurs that they claim white racists use, once again exemplifying psychological projection.

Uncle Tom, Sambo, Coon, House Nigger. These are only some of the approved slanderous words that the cultists actively use against other black people who even slightly question the ideology. In the cult, it is required that we tear down those who leave the congregation to keep everyone else in line. The ideology only works on a population of people where there is an assimilation of thought, standards of discipline for descent and punishment for those who violate the doctrine.

The largest threat to mainstream black ideology is the black conservative, because their existence alone challenges the narrative. When the ideology preaches victimhood, the conservative may say "I don't feel like a victim". When the ideology proclaims that racism affects all black people, the black conservative says, "I am doing fine, and racism doesn't affect me". When the ideology says that you must vote Democrat, the black conservative says, "I'll vote for whoever I want". When the ideology says, "Blackness is your god", the black conservative may say "No, Jesus is my savior".

The black conservative is the rebel who contradicts the ideology and proves that the ideology is flawed. The existence of a counter thought within black culture puts the cult of black ideologues in a quagmire because it risks the exposure of their hypocrisy, exaggerations and false narratives. It becomes imperative that for the cult to survive, the cultists must dismember the black conservative's legitimacy and blackness.

David Webb was not afforded the same legitimacy as his counterpart Reva Martin because of their ideological differences. He is a Conservative; she is a leftist. Her assumptions of his race were dictated by her assumption that a black man could (or should) never be a conservative in principle. Reva's visual unawareness that she was communicating with a black dissident allowed the masses to get a glimpse of how mainstream black ideology functions.

I must emphasize the importance of black legitimization. Once the cult slanders your name, you will never be able to recover. The more famous you are, the more difficult it is to disprove the claims against you. The larger the violation, the closer you move on the scale of racial symmetry to whites. The threat is being removed from the tribe, thus creating an uphill battle to have legitimacy. The mildest criticism of black people - that you believe could ultimately help black people - can land you in the realm of being a "house nigger" or "cooning" for white people. If your critical comments line up with what is perceived as white-thought, then you are merely showing off for your white friends, a.k.a. "cooning" for the white man's approval.

There are trend setters within the community, but they set trends within an already established boundary of what is deemed black. The risk of crossing that line whether it be by means of fashion, music, politics or general criticism can have your blackness permanently challenged. To be a true individual with varied thought, at least publicly, could risk your livelihood and reputation. You will risk being seen as an Oreo, white on the inside and black on the outside. Your blackness is ultimately what is in question if you cross that line. Even with a lifetime of goodwill, one infraction can place you in such an "Oreo" status.

In October 2020, weeks before the 2020 U.S. Presidential Election, rapper and actor Ice Cube decided to utilize his fame to create an initiative to help black people in the United States. He had a plan that he titled "Contract with Black America" which was his attempt to address multiple issues that he felt were hurting the black community including racial inequality, lack of black representation, and lending, judicial, and police reform to name a few.

Whether you agree with what he thinks is important to fix is not the point. The point is that his intentions are coming from a good place. He is attempting to get something done for a community that has constantly been promised prosperity by politicians which disappears for 4 years until they need their illustrious black vote again.

Ice Cube spent a lifetime gaining black notoriety and black legitimacy with his music and movie career. He probably felt he had done enough to present himself as blackness personified but he failed to realize that no one has black immunity once they step across the defined boundaries. Joe Biden and Donald Trump were the final contenders to become the President of the United States and both campaigns contacted him about his Contract for Black America.

Joe Biden's campaign liked his plan but gave the typical Democrat response of "let's talk more after the election". Logically, he went to Donald Trump, who he is no fan of, and asked the campaign if they would be interested in a conversation. Trump's campaign loved his plan and wanted to talk more about it. Once word got out of just a conversation with Donald Trump's campaign, Ice Cube's blackness came under fire.

For the next couple of weeks, Ice Cube went on a media tour to attempt to correct the smears and regain his black legitimacy. The line was drawn by the cultists years ago that Donald Trump was a racist, and the black cult leadership gave no exceptions. Immediately, Ice Cube had to clarify that he was not working directly for Donald Trump, that he was not part of the Trump campaign or is even endorsing Donald Trump. Ice Cube had to go on mainstream stations like CNN to fight the political machine, and he had to go on black oriented programs like Roland Martin Unfiltered Live to attempt to regain his legitimacy.

In a tweet posted by Ice Cube, he stated: "Let me get this straight, I get the president of the United States to agree to put over half a trillion dollars of capital in the Black Community (without an endorsement) and niggas are mad at me?" Ice Cube could not understand why black people were upset when they had the possibility of getting the investment they had been crying about for decades. He failed to understand that they have been trained to believe slogans about change rather than wanting actual change.

He failed to understand that the black elite don't actually want help for the common folk. They want a victim class that they can constantly pick at like vultures on a rotting carcass. The black elite especially don't want help from those that they have deemed as their political enemy. It doesn't matter that 5 years prior, black media looked at Trump like the American dream, took photos with him, laughed with him and admired him. The black political class is overwhelmingly Democrat and proud members of the cult. So once Trump's Presidential run was announced under the opposing Republican party, they unanimously decided to revoke Donald Trump's black goodwill status.

The backlash, or black-lash, was so strong that even Ice Cube had to go on a brief social media hiatus due to the poisonous nature of the black cultists' behavior.

"I know a lot people been wondering where I've been. I was real active before the election, talking about what's needed, you know, specifically for the Black community. About 10 days or two weeks before the election, I pushed back all the way pretty much until now because I just felt there was a lot of noise, a lot of poison, a lot of people with they own agendas—personal agendas or party agendas—and they really wanted to attack me for what I was doing because it was outside of the line of what they was doing, or what they believed need to be done."

Ice Cube even said the words "outside of the line". That line is strictly enforced within the black community, and no one gets a pass. Anyone can be demoted into "Coon of the Year" status - even Ice Cube. Ice Cube's problem is not that he talked to Trump, his problem is that he cares too much about what the cult thinks of him. The problem is that he holds that membership in the cult, no matter how toxic their mindset, to be immensely valuable.

I have no doubt that Ice Cube cares about black people, but he has been blissfully unaware of how poisonous a reaction the black cultists cast towards their defectors. Even though Ice Cube was not purposely attempting to become a defector, he became one, at least in the short term. Only time will tell how well his next album does, or how many black people will want to see the next movie he participates in.

Forced compliance only works if you care about the possible punishment. If you care more about your racial identity than your personal identity, then the cult will always have you enslaved. If you care more about a possible backlash from others rather than how you view yourself, then the cult will continue to win. If only a handful of people cross the boundaries set by black ideologues, then enforcement is swift and easy. However, if there is a massive shift in thought within the "congregation" to the point of not caring what the consequences will be if they leave, then the cult loses its power.

When we see nothing wrong with the lack of a moral compass in our community, we become weak. Cults get their strength in numbers. If black Americans stood up and started questioning things like why we advocate for certain policies, why we support morally corrupt people and why we look up to the black elite when they look down on us, there would be a massive shift felt by every industry. The end result would be the loss of members from the cult of blackness which would strengthen the black individual.

Group-think is not about guidance, it is about obedience. When you are unable to think for yourself and find yourself mimicking the behavior, opinions and outrage of every black person around you, group-think is in full effect. The black community demands assimilation which keeps us stuck. It seems that as a racial minority, we have a sort of obligation to not leave the tribe or question its methods. But we live in a country founded on the principle of individual empowerment rather than waiting to be dictated to.

We should not allow a large government or a hierarchy of black ideologues to determine who we are as individuals. We are tribal creatures, but it doesn't mean that we are incapable of individual thought. There is no problem with feeling a particular kinship with other black people. But when your blackness rules over you like an overbearing king, then you will end up acting like a peasant.

How do you get a group of people to actively accept group-think? You force them together with a group identity, in this case, being black. Next, you emphasize that group-think is imperative to their survival. Without it they risk infiltration. Hence the overreaction of claiming someone is a white sympathizer. The glue that holds black group-think together is victimhood.

The black community romanticizes struggle. We have been conditioned to primarily see the negatives in our past. Or put differently, to interpret our past as primarily being negative. It is the reason why we sometimes measure our blackness by how impoverished we were (or are) and why we laugh off surviving depravity. Within this culture, romance and struggle go hand in hand, which is one of the reasons why black romantic relationships are often primarily about struggle. It's why we look at prisoners as unfortunate recipients of the black struggle rather than willing participants in crime.

If you are black, with both of your parents involved in your childhood, and grew up in a good neighborhood, your blackness meter inches slightly towards whiteness because you lack the struggle of the many and may not have the desire to romanticize it.

This ideology is poisonous because it insidiously holds black people as victims while pretending to empower them. Jim Jones handed his congregation cups filled with Flavor Aid laced with poison so they could die for the cause. We are digesting a less lethal poison called victimhood that causes us to sacrifice ourselves for an invisible cause. When we are handed that cup, we comply because we are not allowed to question what is in it.

To be black in America means that you are allowed to be a victim in every circumstance regardless of who is really responsible. We wear victimhood on our sleeves, which everyone else sees, but they are not allowed to point it out. To be a victim, you have to live a life of low expectations for yourself and for others in your community. Victims are conditioned to see the worst in people and expect to be hurt again. Nothing makes a black person angrier than pointing out that they aren't a victim because they see it as you disregarding their feelings, not as helping them to overcome what is holding them down. Black Americans have lived in this cult for so long that all they see is victimization, and they find it nearly impossible to escape this mindset.

Our ideology has us thinking backwards when we believe that speaking like a victim is black empowerment and speaking like a victor is whiteness. This belief keeps us stuck in the status quo of mediocrity. Defectors like me are at the forefront of the change that is needed to truly help wake up black Americans who are heading down a path which is leading us to hell. It is the strength to resist caring about the smear tactics of the black ideologues that will push us in the direction of victory rather than victimhood.

I am lucky to not have been fully indoctrinated in this cultish ideology even when people close to me were members. Admittingly, there were times in my life when I felt lost and thought that their bible could provide me with something fulfilling. But I quickly realized that their doctrine made me resentful of anyone who wasn't black - even the people that I cared about the most. The constant "woe is me" attitude, the constant highlighting of wrongs from the past, the paranoia of believing that everyone is out to get you, and the constant focus on white people as the end-all-be-all to my existence quickly took a toll on me. The lack of perspective, full scope historical context, and situational nuance and the simplistic world view all played a hand in me quickly returning to my original views.

Without living the life of black indoctrination, I had no true desire to be loved by strangers simply because they happened to look like me. Many black Americans grew up solely around black people, and the thought of having a separation of identity would be like losing an arm. Being black is all they've ever identified with, and the thought of being excommunicated is extremely daunting, which I understand.

Because this was not my existence, the questioning of my blackness was more annoying and laughable than anything else. I have been called a variety of names and had my racial alliance questioned countless times. Yet I still don't care. This is the type of attitude that not only black people, but all people should have when it comes to the attempts to slander you. When you react to the name calling, you give them power over you. I refuse to allow another man or woman to control my feelings by attempting to weaponize my skin color for their own personal gain. This is the mindset of the victor and the mindset that will produce more defectors from the blackness cult.

THE PEOPLE IN BETWEEN – THE LIGHT SKINNED & MIXED-RACE DILEMMA

The use of black identity as our marker for worth has created a dilemma for many Americans. For one, black identity has been used to create hatred toward one another. Darker skinned blacks are pitted against lighter skinned blacks because they represent what they are insecure about, which is being black in general. Those who say "You think you're better than me" to their lighter skinned brethren display a psychological inferiority complex.

Lighter skin, in their mind, represents good and darkness in skin tone represents bad. Consequently, this mindset demonstrates that they feel inferior - even within black society. Those who feel this internalized hatred for their own skin make sure to lash out against those who are lighter in shade. What I find interesting is that the perceived attitude of being better than you for having "good hair", lighter skin, or other European-like features is not what these people put out into the world, it is what is placed onto them by those with a built inferiority complex.

The feelings of inferiority are what drives this animosity within the black community, creating another line of division against us. It is another means of dividing the black community against us.

Challenging one's blackness is challenging one's existence. We cannot help what we are born into, yet the people who are in between are punished for things that they cannot control. The more they look for assimilation with their black brothers and sisters, the more they are either rejected or dismissed as black societal half-breeds. The ones that place these negative perspectives onto lighter skinned blacks and biracial black

Americans are utilizing the same ideological standards that southern leftist democrats instituted for Jim Crow laws.

Jim Crow laws involved a constant recognition of skin color. Jim Crow saw you for what you were outwardly and created a divide based purely on your outward features. There are segments of the black population today that have become the arbiters of the black Jim Crow. Blackness is the determining factor for your importance or dismissal, creating a sliding scale of acceptance the darker the pigmentation. The very people whom we lament as our oppressors for creating a world that judges us because of our pigmentation, are those from whom we are stealing today to determine our cultural acceptance.

This attitude may stem from decades ago when lighter-skinned blacks or bi-racial blacks were seen as more appealing to the white eyes versus the scariness of the feared dark black. Even if this is the case, it is our responsibility to stop the cycle of inner hatred, not perpetuate it. The pain from the lack of acceptance within white society has turned into resentment against the ones who were accepted. Darker skinned blacks may see themselves as rejected in comparison to lighter skinned blacks.

Whether it stems from race mixing due to a master-slave relationship over a century ago or a loving bi-racial relationship, the interruption of black-African lineage with European lineage is what becomes insulting to the so-called pure breed darker skinned black who is insulted by the existence of these people.

I speak of the struggle for light-skinned people because no one else does. They are seen as people with privilege based on their perceived acceptance within white society, but we lack the understanding that for many light-skinned blacks and mixed-raced blacks, this attitude has created a void for them because they are not accepted by either side. They become the people who are in between.

They are not embraced by black society, nor are they by white society. They are given privilege when they do not feel privileged. Humans are social creatures who want some form of group acceptance, or in this case, racial acceptance. For many of these people, they lack identity, and they are pushed into the void of an increasingly over racialized society.

I met someone who lives in between racial identities. Her name is Zyalena Blackwood. Zyalena, is a mixed-race woman created by a black father and mixed-race mother. Zyalena was adopted at an early age by a white family in South Dakota. Growing up in a white family for her was never about race within the home, it was about morals and how you treat others, but she could not shake the fact that she was different from everyone else.

Based on superficial appearance, she was not quite black, and she was not quite white, she was quintessentially in between. Depending on her hairstyle, she could pass for either race. Occasionally strangers would play guessing games about her cultural background.

Throughout grade school, she had leftist white teachers who thought they were helping by pointing out racial differences but who actually created even more of a division between her and her classmates. The indoctrination about the societal superiority of whites and the preaching of victimhood to any non-white placed her into an even greater void, never feeling fully accepted by whites and being dismissed by the black population.

From the standards of the leftist blacks that she would encounter, she was not black and was not allowed to call herself such a thing. She could merely be called the vague term "woman of color", which is the politically correct way of dismissing the "other" into an identity box that you can cast to the side. What is a woman of color? Essentially nothing, it is just a label and a bad label at that. Clearly, she is a woman, but what cultural identity does the word "color" represent? The answer is nothing, it is just a filler title indicating that she really didn't fit in anywhere.

After grade school, like many young people, she was constantly trying to discover who she was, and racial identity came into play for her. Her situation of being adopted and then adding to the complexity of racial identity within America was a compounding effect that led her to feel disconnected from any particular group, creating a life of internal solitude. She belonged with no one, and she was wanted by no one.

For many years she loathed her skin because it was not definitive enough. She hated the void of racial existence that she was shoved into due to her blackness only being partial. She struggled with loving herself throughout most of her life because it is difficult to love yourself when it feels like the world does not love you. Her desperation to have her blackness recognized was halted by the toxic culture of the sliding scale of blackness importance: the lighter, the least.

Now as a mother in her early 30s, she is starting to pick up the pieces of her self-esteem so she can move forward in her life. She is slowly overcoming the rejection that she endured as an adopted mixed-race woman, but it is a scar that she will probably carry for the rest of her life. The pain that she endured emotionally is because of black culture's adoption of leftistized racial segregation. She was scolded for her so-called "light skinned privilege" without actually being or feeling privileged.

These leftist tactics victimized her throughout her life, and she is now realizing that this virus runs throughout the black community. This mentality chews away at our prefrontal cortex, so we do not pay attention to the pain that we are causing others. We celebrate our illusionary handicap as a point of pride and cheer for more black-identarian dogma in our lives. If this continues, we will create more people like Zyalena who will live without racial acceptance and create increasing resentment.

– CHAPTER 6 –

THE MENTALITY OF THE VICTIM

A victim is defined as someone who has been subjected to oppression, hardship or mistreatment. Black Americans have been set up as America's victim, and there are examples of actual discrimination that were co-signed by the government throughout American history. I will never deny the existence of discrimination. But much of what we call discrimination today is based on interpretation that is influenced by our internal biases.

If you are a member of the cult of blackness, you have been inundated with historical references that we are told equate with the actions of the present. Your default thought process is to see color and then see a victim because being black and being a victim go hand in hand. Within the cult you are taught that blackness is a strength but also inherently weak against its white oppressor. We are told that as long as black people are in a white majority nation, blacks will always be victims of the white majority's alleged deep-seated hatred.

This collective mindset of being America's perpetual victim drags black people down like an anchor. This mindset keeps us complacent about our culture's ill behavior. We are reluctant to advise other victims that they should change. There are even very successful blacks that lean on victimhood when they find it useful.

Successful black people will repeat cult phrases like "I had to work twice as hard to get half as far" but anyone, regardless of race, who is successful has to work hard. How are you measuring your hard work? Are we to assume that successful white, Hispanic, Asians and Africans don't work hard to become successful? You get in what you put out, especially in a place like America where meritocracy is more important than race.

Companies that hire purely based on race and don't have the backing of the government, don't last. It is not profitable to racially discriminate because competency and efficiency keep a company running properly. The notion that you must work twice as hard only instills a sense of insecurity in the job market for black people and allows them to make excuses when they fail.

The cult leadership has told us that the successful black people are the ones that somehow slipped through the cracks because victims rarely succeed. The cult leadership has convinced black Americans that their destiny relies on the philanthropy of white people rather than our own individual strength to overcome our personal trials. The low expectations of the cult have seeped into the psyche of the black congregation. Leftists are convinced that the fuel to drive us forward is their condescending pity.

It is a strong claim to make when I say that the majority of black Americans act as if or believe that they are in some way a victim. There are various areas in which we can see this attitude of victimhood. Let's start with affirmative action. The idea of giving preferential treatment to black people, not because they are the most qualified but to meet a racial quota should be insulting. But to a victim it is laudable. The idea that we need quotas implies that we could never compete with non-blacks and thus we need leftist policies to give us a handout because we are incapable otherwise.

Affirmative action advocates have even gone as far as lowering their SAT standards for entry into certain colleges to get more black faces on their campus. In an article by the New York Post titled "Harvard's gatekeeper reveals SAT cutoff scores based on race", they detail their discrimination against whites and Asians and their lowering of standards for Blacks, Hispanics, and native Americans.

"He (William Fitzsommons, Dean of Admissions for Harvard) said Harvard sends recruitment letters to African-American, Native American and Hispanic high schoolers with mid-range SAT scores, around 1100 on math and verbal combined out of a possible 1600, CNN reported. Asian-Americans only receive a recruitment letter if they score at least 250 points higher — 1350 for women, and 1380 for men."

Changing the rules to incorporate more black faces only sounds enticing if you are riddled with victimhood and full of excuses as to why you are incapable of competing. If you are black, are you okay with universities implying that to get more black people, they have to dumb down their acceptance standards? How would you feel if you were accepted into a college, and you knew they practiced methods of affirmative action? Wouldn't you question your eligibility?

Lowering expectations for the purpose of racial inclusion is like opportunity welfare. This sort of racial inclusion sacrifices self-esteem, personal honor and fortitude and will only widen the scar that victimhood leaves behind. My criticism about affirmative action is not just about whether it works, which is debatable, but also about how this type of policy contributes to the spread of victimhood within black culture and leftist circles.

"Too often the result of affirmative action has been an artificial diversity that gives the appearance of parity between blacks and whites that has not yet been achieved in

reality...Preferences tend to attack one form of discrimination with another...Affirmative action encourages a victim-focused identity, and sends the message that there is more power in our past suffering than in our present achievements." – Shelby Steele

This bigotry of low expectations towards black people in America is overwhelmingly unhelpful and encourages us to make excuses for some of our failures. We tell ourselves that black criminals are incarcerated because of a legacy of slavery. Black children fail in public schools because of a legacy of segregation. Black urban poverty is due to a legacy of urban redlining. These historical mentions become the excuses for our lack of achievement. We accept the belief that we cannot overcome such a legacy without the intervention of various institutions, especially the government.

Victims always want the support of others because they don't believe that they can survive alone. We believe that we are so in need of saving that we are heading into the arms of what has caused us the most pain - the government. We want to "save" our black men in prison by advocating for softer penalties for criminal offenses instead of fairer penalties. In some circles, they want the abolition of prisons entirely. We want to view adults who made personal decisions to violate the rule of law to be treated as victims because they may have grown up in a harsh environment. We have decided to treat adults as babies who are incapable, so we must bend the rules, lower the expectations and ignore the people whom they have hurt to end up incarcerated in the first place. The alleged "victims" who were caught dealing drugs were poisoning a community of people that we claim to care about. We show more concern for men who chose to physically harm other human-beings than for their victims.

While these men chose to commit the crimes, this does not mean that they should be treated with disdain. There is a serious issue in America with criminal recidivism, and this is partly because of the lack of opportunities presented to them once they leave jail. There are obviously issues with our laws that make damn near anything a felony and create future employment very difficult for those who are trying to avoid returning to the criminal world. There are imbalances between penalties for cocaine and crack that are disproportionate and should be addressed. And there is a lack of rehabilitation and training within prisons to help reintroduce these people into civil society.

There are legitimate concerns surrounding laws and incarceration within America, but this does not make these people victims. Unless we are claiming that a significant number of people who are locked up are actually innocent, we have to acknowledge that these people made bad choices that landed them in such a situation. When we attempt to make victims out of the guilty, we are removing their accountability for their actions. Using excuses of an awful childhood, poverty or racism is simply a crutch for their individual mistakes.

We have made victims out of even the wealthiest and the most fortunate black Americans to have ever existed. For example, the #OscarsSoWhite campaign was created to complain about the lack of black representation in the Oscars. Why are we making victims out of the most privileged black people to ever exist? Why do we assume that because they didn't receive a statue from a white majority Academy of Motion Pictures, that it invalidates their talents? Why do we need such validation when we have a plethora of black oriented award shows? Are we devaluing our own to place ourselves in the position of victims when we don't receive what we perceive as fairness from a white majority society?

It is possible that our lack of Oscar success today is partly race related but also keep in mind that blacks are also competing with a white majority population. I think sometimes we forget black people are only 13% of the American population, and there aren't that many black actors at the extreme levels of talent to compete with a wider pool of white talent.

The activists are correct. The Oscars are so white but due mostly to having a greater population of white individuals who are interested in acting and are talented. If racial disparities are the end all be all for claims of discrimination, then where are the #NBAsoBlack activists? Since the year 2000, there have only been 2 white NBA MVPs, this must be due to the discrimination of white people within the NBA ranks, right? Or is it possible that talent rises to the top and the talent and interest in basketball by white Americans is not as high?

The mentality of the victim has no boundaries as far as who can claim victimhood. Prisoners who have lost everything including their freedom are victims to a racist society. At the same time ultra-wealthy Hollywood elites are victims to the even wealthier white elite within Hollywood. Anyone can be a victim if they choose to wear that badge and live a life of manufacturing an endless number of excuses for their personal failures and the failures of those like them.

What I find to be the most detrimental part of the victim mentality is when it is transferred to our black children. This gives them a head start in clinging to life's disappointments. Imagine being told at a young age that no matter how hard you work, no matter how much money you make and no matter how good your character is, that most of the people you encounter will only see you as just another nigger. Imagine having an adult explain that your trust should only go as far as the skin color of the person you're encountering because the opposing complexion is untrustworthy.

One of my earliest memories was when someone close to me told me point blank, "You can't trust white people." I don't remember my exact age when this was explained to me, but I was old enough to see the hypocrisy of trust based on race. I knew black people who did reprehensible things, yet I was supposed to only trust people who look like me? Wouldn't it be wiser to trust people who are trustworthy? Regardless of this faulty logic, this is the type of rhetoric that easily spreads throughout black homes across the country, and it only contributes to the victim mentality.

What if I didn't question this terrible logic? What if I bought the narrative of inherent black victimhood? Would you be surprised if I had low self-esteem? Would you be shocked if I had little success in life?

If you give someone a constant message of low worth, they will live a lifestyle of low worth. If you view black people as the constant victim, they will live the lifestyle of the victim. If you tell a child that they are a victim before they even get a chance to experience life, you are handicapping their potential for personal excellence.

As important as the narrative that is preached to children is the behavior that is exhibited by their parents and influential adult figures. Children mimic the behavior of the adults that they hold in high regard, making them easily susceptible to copying both positive and negative behavioral traits. We need to be cognizant about how we carry ourselves around our children. If we act as victims our children will by osmosis become the victims of the next generation.

With every generation of black children comes a greater opportunity for them to shed the destructive behavior of the previous generation. However, we have been stifling this progress with constant indoctrination with black victim narratives at home and a leftist victim ideology in our public schools. Our kids are being taught that their value and life predictors are based purely on the color of their skin and not the content of their character.

They have leftist teachers who place posters on their walls with images of Martin Luther King Jr. while teaching their students an opposing message to that of Dr King. Just as terrible as what they are doing to black children, these teachers are also victimizing white children by telling them that they are born with a privilege that they didn't even ask for and that they must apologize for. These teachers are also telling their white students that they must endure masochism as they suffer for the sins of white men and women from the past. They are told to be less white because their whiteness is stealing from their black classmates.

Everyone has their own reasons why they believe they are victims or preach victimhood to others. Some of these preachers love the clout of acting as the savior for the victimized and feeling morally righteous as they stand above their victim to lend them a hand, much like the teachers I described. Some preach victimhood for attention or like some members of the media-class, for ratings. Some people want to become victims because it is far easier to lay blame at someone else's feet than be accountable for their situation. I often say "human-beings don't do things for no reason", meaning there is always a motivating factor behind our actions, and this is no different with the preaching of victimhood.

Victims want to constantly be heard about what ails them without seeking a tangible resolution because the point isn't to problem solve but to complain. This desperation, complaining, and drama affects those in their proximity with their negativity.

Why is having a victim mentality bad? First, being a victim puts you in a position of powerlessness and an inability to change your circumstances. If you are powerless to change, then you need someone else to help you. Powerlessness can make you dependent and constant powerlessness is a character weakness. Weak people may garner empathy, but no one truly respects them.

The second reason is that being a victim means that there is always an oppressor, and these victims aren't gun-shy about who they target as their oppressor. The metaphorical gun is their finger pointing at someone else to blame them for their personal flaws. Everyone is responsible for their outcome except for them. The greater the victim mentality, the more oppressors that they can list. The unfortunate outcome of such a variety of supposed oppressors is that they are undoubtedly mis-characterizing individuals or groups of people. Ironically this creates actual victims due to the mischaracterization resulting from their slander.

The last reason that a victim mentality is bad is that it is almost always used to either subjugate people or to create a division between groups of people. In the case of black Americans, it has been used to hold us down long enough to accept alleged help from the government, the leftist elite, and your everyday narcissist with a savior complex. In exchange for their perceived help, we must vote for them, buy from them and applaud the illusion of their selflessness. If you attempt to stray away from their subjugation, then they will enforce tactics that result in racial division.

The victim mentality always sees life as a struggle between opposing forces. Victim versus oppressor. Black versus white. Democrat versus Republican. Leftist versus conservative. Tolerant versus racist. These counter forces are used to divide people into smaller and more controllable groups, making life all about us versus them and asking everyone to choose sides. Racial division is one of the strongest methods of keeping black people submissive and making them fearful of straying from the accepted narrative. If you were to realize that your white neighbor has more in common with you than you have been told, then you could come together and fight against the morally corrupt who are actively manipulating the American population for their own gain. Racial division builds a fence between you and your white neighbor because you perceive them as strangers.

When Joe Biden went on "The Breakfast Club" radio show and said, "*If you have a problem figuring out whether you're for me or Trump, then you ain't black*", he was using racial identity to put blacks into a political camp. He and others like him know they can get away with these statements because we view ourselves as political victims and act as racial identitarians. This combination makes us easily swayed by racialized political pandering.

Using Biden's logic, voting against him means you oppose black interest or that you're not actually "black". He is actively muddying the waters between blackness as a complexion and blackness as an ideology. This utilization of a consistent "us versus them" slogan with black Americans only works because many of us have been trained to be victims.

Joe Biden would never dream of going on an Asian oriented radio programming and saying "You ain't Asian" because that would be seen as extremely insulting, however for black people, we somehow agree that it's perfectly fine for someone outside of our racial group to determine who we are, what we do or who we vote for as a collective when this expectation does not exist in other racial groups within America.

Manipulation is repeatedly used to incorporate a victim mindset into your daily routine. You are no longer in control because there is always someone pulling your leash in one direction or the other. Black people think that being considered as a group should appease us, but in reality, it leads us to chase the desired stick thrown by our societal masters.

We chase the stick when they give us a special exemption, when they suggest giving us a day off from work on Martin Luther King Jr. day, and when they promise grand proposals like reparations. Manipulators know how to give us temporary satisfaction in exchange for long-term obedience, and they specialize in distracting us from focusing on their devilish ways by pretending to be our angels.

The manipulators want us to approach the world from the perspective of looking up and waiting for their next command. They constantly starve us of genuine opportunities and beat us down with victim narratives, yet we are supposed to be happy to fetch their slippers with momentary glee as soon as they talk about the "struggle of the black man." These people have no interest in changing the social state of black Americans because they won't allow for a change to the mental state of black Americans. Instead, they refer to you as a victim and never call black people what they truly are - survivors.

The word survive is defined as to carry on despite hardships or trauma. Being a survivor is inspirational, and it exemplifies perseverance. Stories of survival motivate people to do better for themselves and become examples of how personal strength and a will to live can move you past victimization. As survivors is how I view black people throughout American history, and you should too. There are many examples of black Americans being victimized. But they overcame and became survivors despite such victimization.

A survivor is free from manipulation and has mental independence. A survivor does not need a hand to hold to lift him up. A survivor can do it himself because of having overcome many other obstacles before. A survivor does not remain cemented at her current place in life because she is free to move forward as she pleases. Survivors don't have time to make excuses for failures because they see them as unproductive in reaching their ultimate agenda. Survivors don't beg to be heard or seen because they already command respect.

Ask yourself these questions: Do you want to be a victim who complains about what has not been fairly given to you or a survivor who makes life work for them? Do you want to constantly feel oppressed, or do you want to overcome? Do you want to weakly depend on others, or do you want to strengthen your resiliency against trials? Do you want to be a slave to the condescending hand that feeds you? Do you want our new leftist saviors to rescue you or do you want to walk past them and save yourself? No one can promise that you will never be victimized, but you can have control over if you view yourself as a survivor.

CHAPTER 7

IVORY TOWER BLACK ELITES

"There is another class of coloured people who make a business of keeping the troubles, the wrongs, and the hardships of the Negro race before the public. Having learned that they are able to make a living out of their troubles, they have grown into the settled habit of advertising their wrongs — partly because they want sympathy and partly because it pays. Some of these people do not want the Negro to lose his grievances, because they do not want to lose their jobs."

– Booker T. Washington

"My Larger Education"

(1911)

There is a class of black Americans who are unelected yet feel that they can speak for their black "constituents". The average black person may not envision these representatives as being part of an elite class, but they are in every measurement part of the social, economic and media elite. They are some of the wealthiest and most influential Americans and they have an audience that is easily swayed by their comments. The black elites of America are the leaders and financiers of the modern black ideological cult. Without their influence, the gospel of victimhood would not be nearly as prevalent in American society as it is currently.

The purpose of black leadership within America is not to lead but to mislead. Their objective is to deflect criticisms, repeat a narrative and find a way to profit from the fear that dwells in the black American psyche. They all have their hands in the pot of black fear, and they cash in on their prize routinely.

The black elites of America are among some of the most disingenuous people in this country. They mask their greed for power with their supposed goal of black assimilation while pretending to be suffering in luxury. They have no problem misleading black Americans into believing that they too are being restricted when in actuality their life has been nothing but a highway of opportunity.

"We're literally hunted EVERYDAY/EVERYTIME we step foot outside the comfort of our homes! Cannot even go for a damn jog man! Like WTF man are you kidding me?!?!?!?!?!? No man for real ARE YOU KIDDING ME!!!!! I'm sorry Ahmaud (Rest In Paradise)" – LeBron James via Twitter

LeBron James tweeted this misleading message declaring that all black people are in danger when he lives in constant comfort. A man who has spent his entire adulthood surrounded by wealth and protection has no problem pretending that he is experiencing danger himself when one of us dies. He's allowed to feel empathetic - no one will take that from him. But he is spreading a message of fear to millions of people without any hesitation. He is projecting an overly emotional message in order for his followers to keep their attention on what he has to sell, black virtue.

When LeBron tweets to millions of Americans stating that black Americans are being hunted, he is setting a stage where fear is the motivating factor for black Americans to react in a manner that benefits him. Regardless of his wealth, LeBron needs notoriety and black legitimacy to continue to profit from the average American. As long as he appears to be a conscious "brother" and aware of the struggle, we will kindly ignore his wealth and the possibility that he is using our emotions against us.

The elite have a habit of proclaiming their elegance to the common man, employing bamboozling narratives and then profiting from our confusion. This is no different with the black elite. The danger that Lebron states is lurking in the streets, if were true, would not affect him. Lebron is not scared of being pulled over by the police - because they are escorting him. Lebron is concerned about being chased down by white people while jogging, but it would only be because they want an autograph. Lebron has no legitimate fear of danger in his daily life, but he has no problem making sure that the rest of the black non-millionaires live in a state of paranoia.

While having wealth beyond what most people in this world could ever dream of, LeBron is still in need of public clout. He is a public figure and the imagery of him as the good guy activist gives him that extra edge when we are deciding which basketball jersey to buy and which pair of sneakers to wear. Ultimately, the manufactured image of black advocacy is what he seeks to profit financially in the long run.

Throughout his illustrious career, he has discovered a way to monetize black tragedy by using black activism. It costs LeBron nothing to write a tweet about a racialized incident or mention his feelings of alleged racism when a reporter sticks a microphone in his face. His advocacy makes him appear as the "Black Batman", ready to swoop down from his ivory tower and save us from sinister characters. But we forget that Bruce Wayne was also part of the elite class.

Being rich does not mean that you don't have a conscience or that you are unable to care about people who are less fortunate, however when you are wealthy and you find ways to monetize your concern, then I am skeptical of what you really care about. LeBron has all the opportunity to help black Americans in any way he chooses to, yet he always finds ways to yell fire in the movie theater. He has the resources and connections to create organizations that help people quietly, but he wants to make sure you know how charitable he is.

Not every charity is equal, and not every charitable person has the intent to help. People like LeBron know how to monetize a problem without really looking for a solution because if it were fixed, it would limit his revenue stream. If LeBron could flip a switch and stop racism, do you think he would turn it off? Why would he? He's gained so much political power and public attention by being one of the black elite spokespersons. When he and his Miami Heat teammates took a photo wearing hoodies in tribute to the death of Trayvon Martin, he was lauded as a black hero and given the untouchable title of activist.

As one of the leaders of the cult, he has no interest in addressing real issues that affect many black Americans because that would mean that he would be highlighting what we keep hidden from outsiders and from ourselves. Attempting to resolve issues like broken families, lack of male masculinity, and our lack of concern over black-on-black death could portray black Americans in a negative light. But it might also begin to improve our life situation.

The elite avoid these topics to not disrupt the status quo of degradation within the black community across this country. They also avoid these topics because they understand that the majority of black Americans have no appetite to air out their dirty laundry in front of white people. This is a mutually beneficial agreement in which both parties are fine with avoiding valid attempts to address solvable issues and instead accept rare racially ambiguous encounters as the black man's true plight.

LeBron James can call himself a civil rights activist who has no problem pointing the finger at our supposed racist society that he says is methodically executing black people on a daily basis. But he remains silent when it comes to the Chinese Communist Party (CCP) that is actually enslaving an ethnic minority for the purpose of re-education, slave labor, harvesting organs, forced abortions and murder when necessary.

LeBron has no problem profiting from a country that is actually committing the same atrocities that he claims are happening in America. Because of this, we have to question his true intentions. We have to point out the hypocrisy of LeBron stating that white America looks the other way when black people are being killed when he's actively looking the other way when there is a genocide being committed in a country from which he directly profits. If our history of ethnic enslavement is something we should constantly talk about in America, why is it okay for it to be ignored in China, LeBron?

The elite can get away with promoting false narratives and painting themselves with racial justice imagery because the requirements to do so are extremely few in America. All you need to do is change your Twitter bio to state the word "activist". To appease black Americans as a true hero of racial justice, you just need to claim that you are one. It doesn't require any plausible action or tangible results. All that needs to be done is that you are occasionally vocal, and you will receive the adulation of the many. The elite are aware of this ratio of low effort to high profit, so they are far too willing to implement this methodology even if the byproduct is more racial tension and more racial division.

Not all the elite are the mega-wealthy like LeBron James. However they are generally far wealthier and influential than the average black American. Many of these men and women make a great living as high-ranking members of the black ideological cult who pretend to fight for the common black American while actually lining their pockets. These people understand the playbook far better than anyone else and have the resources to exploit black America without conscience. Al Sharpton, Jesse Jackson, Louis Farrakhan and Benjamin Crump are just a few of the prominent alleged black civil rights provocateurs. These men have spent decades standing at podiums attempting to represent what black Americans think, want and feel to such a great degree that white Americans actually believe them.

The civil rights elite are a special class of elite because they are extremely good at what they do. They rub elbows with the most powerful politicians in the country, like the Clintons and other prominent Democrats. They are capable of organizing with many of the captains of industries in America. They are featured on network television stations like CNN and MSNBC as guests who are able to spread their narrative to millions of viewers with ease. They are capable of captivating the black mind with a fear narrative before that mind is even able to decide for itself.

If there is a racialized incident that becomes highlighted in the media, the black civil rights elite have the connections to make sure that this story continues to command coverage. Once the public believes the narrative set forward, they will reap the benefits of our overreaction and hypersensitivity. If new evidence comes out that disproves their narrative, they and the media have no problem pretending that it doesn't exist with the intention to keep us emotionally outraged.

For example, when Michael Brown was shot and killed by Officer Darren Wilson, the rumor spread that Michael had his hands up yet was still shot. "Hands Up, Don't Shoot" was the chosen slogan plastered on TV, printed on shirts, and yelled at rallies. And it was the motivation for the destructive riots in Ferguson, Missouri.

What many Americans don't know is that when the U.S. Department of Justice came to investigate the incident, Michael Brown's friend, Dorian Johnson, admitted that he lied about Michael Brown's hands being raised in a surrendering fashion. But at that point, it didn't matter. The lie was already believed. The fear was spread. And the profits were cashed in.

The people today that we call "Civil Rights Leaders" are not leaders, nor do they act in a civil manner. Their promotion of racial hatred and animosity is the polar opposite of civility. If anything, these people are Civil Rights Misleaders because all they do is sway black America into believing the unprovable, hide evidence that could promote a peaceful outcome, and make false equations to historical wrongs. Al Sharpton is at the top of the list as a multi-decade civil rights misleader whose behavior has led to riots and accusations of racism which have destroyed the lives of black Americans and black communities.

The Tawana Brawley rape allegation incident in 1971 brought Al Sharpton to national prominence with his bombastic advocacy in defense of Tawana, regardless of the fact that there was no evidence backing up her allegations. We all know today that Tawana made up the lie of being raped and evidence shows that she had racial slurs written on her body to propagate racial intent for her false claim.

Al Sharpton is an alleged minister who is willing to slander anyone as a racist without a second thought and destroy the livelihood of anyone who stands in his way. For a man of God, he is ruthless in his pursuit of power and does not care about the aftermath of his actions.

Al Sharpton is correct when he yells "No justice, no peace" because he is not interested in justice nor peace. Peace doesn't make him money, victims do. Black victimization is necessary for his pursuit of power and fuels the donations for his, in my opinion, slush-fund non-profit National Action Network.

Based on the Nation Action Network's publicly accessible 990 Tax Form filed for 2019, they stated that in 2018 they had taken in $7,313,170 in donations and claimed that $7,028,833 went towards NAN's expenses. What did they do with that money? 41.1% of the claimed $7,028,833 of expenses went towards salaries and compensation, of which Al Sharpton paid himself $1,046,948. 58.8% of the $7,028,833 went towards "other expenses". I'm no financial savant, but it doesn't sound like there was much room for money to go towards any programs to help the people he claims to advocate for.

Despite his crooked behavior, he's able to get away consistently unscathed because everyone is too afraid to speak up about his greed for fear of being seen as hurting one of the leaders of the cult. Al Sharpton can brush off the many lies he has spread throughout the decades because his words were supposedly in pursuit of helping black Americans. In this cult, all you need is for people to believe that you have the intention to help. Results are optional.

August 23rd, 2020, civil rights lawyer Benjamin Crump made a statement via Twitter: *"Wow. This Black man was shot several times in the back by @KenoshaPolice today. He was getting into his car after apparently breaking up a*

fight between two women. He's in critical condition now. We demand JUSTICE!
#BlackLivesMatter."

This was a tweet that was shared by over 70 thousand people with the intention to mislead. The intention was to create a narrative of innocence rather than being factual regarding what actually happened. Misdirection regarding these incidents needed to sway black people. The congregation of black ideologues will always take the side of black people if the opposition is an authority figure or white. The black elite know that this is a vulnerability that we are not willing to repair because it is part of our cult's doctrine.

Benjamin Crump purposefully failed to mention the reason Jacob Blake was even there, because it would interfere with his manufacturing of a narrative for the public. Benjamin Crump doesn't want you to know that Jacob Blake had a warrant for his arrest for sexual assault and that the home where the shooting took place was that of the same black woman whom he had allegedly assaulted before, and that he had come there to violate her again.

Benjamin didn't want you to know that Jacob resisted arrest multiple times and had a weapon on him. Benjamin especially doesn't want you to know that the car he was attempting to get into wasn't even his car, it was his victim's car. When you learn all these facts, it paints a very different picture of the man you are heralding as a victim of racial injustice. Instead, you see him for what he actually is - a terrorist of the black community.

Civil Rights Activists find victims in criminals because they have more conflicts with the police. The activists would be waiting a long time to try to profit off of a truly innocent black person who was not in the process of committing a crime, didn't have a warrant and wasn't resisting an arrest which resulted in their death.

The black elite must be able to maximize profits, even if that means that they have to cut some corners by propping up clearly flawed black men to inflate the danger that presents itself in the average black American's life. To be blunt, the modern civil rights activist today acts like an ambulance chaser searching for their next client.

Blended into the occupation of civil rights activists are the black intellectual elite who focus more on messaging than marching. These are the men and women who have sat in a classroom longer than any of us to hold more legitimacy over their potential detractors. These people not only impress black Americans, but all Americans because they have proven themselves in the world of academia by holding titles of professors and authors like Michael Eric Dyson, Ibram X. Kendi and Cornel West.

The average person experiences intellectual insecurity when they encounter someone with such academic esteem, so we tend to cower rather than challenge. Because of this intimidation factor, black intellectuals who gain national attention rarely have their rhetoric challenged publicly. These are men and women who know how to weaponize race with such ease and intellectual acumen that we dare not challenge them for fear of receiving an epic verbal lashing.

Understandably, black people are proud to see other black people who are doing well for themselves, especially because they know that many of us struggle on a daily basis. The rarity of not only having a black college professor but one who teaches at a highly esteemed university is no doubt impressive. However, our impressionability with black accomplishment is another vulnerability that the black elites exploit for their personal benefit.

The black intellectual elite are among the most dangerous men and women in America because they use their academic credentials to cause the average person to question themselves when presented with complex information. These are extremely intelligent people who spend hours theorizing about reality to create fiction.

The more theoretical they are, the more they deviate from factional information. They are also dangerous because they are arrogant in their certainty and will fight adamantly to prove that they are right. They have no problem with pointing out the inaccuracies of others but show no humility when you attempt to dismantle their arguments.

I have watched countless hours of footage with Michael Eric Dyson speaking to the average man with such convoluted word usage that they are unable to detect his bullshit. He understands that his words allow for confusion, and this uncertainty about the ideas of someone with academic credentials sadly leads us to be impressed rather than skeptical.

Michael Eric Dyson's strategy is to throw an onslaught of words that don't appear to go together, and while we are stuck trying to put together the meaning of his verbal vomit, he has already crossed the finish line while watching us squirm. He has impressively mastered the art of confusion to keep us compliant. His vocabulary usage in combination with the speed at which he can regurgitate his statements is his main tactic that puts the average person into mental submission.

A mistake that we often make as people is that we believe that a person's ability to speak a particular language equates to that person's intelligence or legitimacy, so we are easily impressed when someone can spit out rarely used vocabulary. While it does take a particular level of intelligence to engage in this behavior, studying a dictionary is not a high-level function.

Con artists play on the emotions of people and understand that the perception of their high intelligence will produce little resistance to their ultimate motive. It's no different from the intellectual elite who gain power, notoriety, and wealth based on their perceived intelligence. Their understanding of the average person's intellectual insecurity benefits them in the long run. In the meanwhile, we get tricked into believing what they want us to believe.

The motive of the black intelligentsia is to spread and profit from the fear of black victimization from a white society. They have the power to not only get a public platform on network television, but to consistently teach American youth about all the ills of American history and how this continues to occur today. They are able to infect the minds of young adults with the verbiage of black victimhood on a daily basis, without pushback. The black intellectual elite are at best theorists, not problem solvers.

Many of the black intellectual elite are also believers in the teachings of critical race theory, which tells Americans that every system in our country has been designed to oppress minorities in favor of the white majority. But no one highlights how these same critics are flourishing within these systems. Funny how a system that is designed to crush black people allows for these particular black people to make it to the highest institutions and become some of the most influential people in America.

Are we to believe that the system just had a flaw to let them slip through the cracks or is it possible that they know that their dedication to education and persistence in personal betterment were the key factors for them to achieve success that most people are unable to reach regardless of race?

It is the scam of victimhood that they are selling, and unfortunately many of us are buying it wholesale. They want us to believe that they were the lucky ones who all the racist systems accidentally overlooked so that we stay as the unfortunate ones off of whom they prey. Who else will buy their books, pay to see their lectures, and watch their television programming? It is the poor people whom they say are incapable of reaching their own level of personal success.

It is no different from someone selling the idea of how you can become rich - just buy their book and join their program. The people that fall for this scam never become rich and they suffer because they don't question what is being sold to them. Likewise, black Americans never improve their life standards after buying from the black intellectual because all they have to sell is the promotion of victim complexes.

For these professional theorists, their educational resume gives them credibility so that they can make all of their claims that everyone, everything, everywhere is indeed racist. They tell us that we have been fooled into accepting white racist patriarchy that oppresses our black souls under the destructive force of white superiority.

Oprah Winfrey has even joined in on the black victim gravy train by convincing her mostly white audience that they are part of the problem:

"There are white people who are not as powerful as the system of white people, the caste system that has been put in place but they still, no matter where they are on the rung or the ladder of success will have their whiteness".

This is all said as white faces unquestioningly nod with affirmation about how they are privileged and become magically convinced that they must be racist.

There must have been a major screw up in our American caste system to have allowed this one black woman to climb from poverty to becoming a multi-billionaire with the full acceptance of all racial groups in America. It is almost like Oprah is purposely exaggerating how a caste system operates because if she did know, she couldn't make this claim. If we did have a true caste system, you would never have heard the name Oprah unless you were her neighbor.

I also think that Oprah speaks this leftist jargon to keep the political left from chastising her for her hard-earned riches. Even Oprah will engage in the lies and deception to cash in on the victim narrative and deflect criticism.

Even someone like Jamelle Hill, a millionaire, in the sports media landscape gained more notoriety the more she pushed the narrative of black victimhood within a white majority society. The more money she made from big deal contracts with ESPN, the more left-leaning she became, pushing this victim narrative to a class of people that are well below her tax-bracket. Even in athletics, an arena that celebrates the best in people, she finds a way to reduce it to the lowest denominator by always bringing it back to race:

"Some black students feel safer, both physically and emotionally, on an HBCU campus — all the more so as racial tensions have risen in recent years. Navigating a predominantly white campus as a black student can feel isolating, even for athletes."

Even in a situation when a boxing match between a white boxer, Jake Paul, and former NBA player, Nate Robinson, resulted in Jake Paul knocking out Nate Robinson, Jemele Hill couldn't help herself by bringing up race in a contest where the best athlete happened to be white.

During an interview with Jake Paul on the VICE television show "Cari & Jemele", Jemele Hill regurgitates her racial nonsense directly at Jake Paul:

"Listen, it's a sensitive time right now. We just had to witness a white man knock out a black man smooth out in front of all of America, and that's why I asked that."

The list can go on and on about these people who live in ivory towers while forcing a narrative down America's throat about how they are either a victim or an oppressor. All of these people are extremely wealthy, powerful and have the means to spread a message whenever it suits their purposes. They are the black aristocrats who occasionally mingle with the common folk as long as they can benefit from such exposure.

These people do not want us to consider their bank statements as a motive when they use language that is divisive. If we tear each other apart, limb by limb, they will be unaffected by the destruction that has ensued. They will help us identify our oppressors, place them on a stake and flick the lighter. And the elite will smirk in delight that they aren't the ones awaiting this fate. It is all a distraction, and it has always been this way.

Powerful rich people don't take kindly to losing either money or influence. Social currency along with monetary currency are extremely valuable to them and it affords them the ability to act as chameleons when we are looking for the culprits in our social confusion.

The average white person does not lose sleep thinking about black people, and the sooner black people understand this as a reality, the sooner we can move on with our lives. This battling between commoners of a different complexion and ethnicity is a social manipulation propagated by the elite class.

It is clear that the elite come in a variety of shades and from either sex, but they have one major agenda and that's for you not to see them for who they truly are. If you can focus on race, then you'll never see their class.

- CHAPTER 8 -

RACISM AND SUPREMACY

"The most damage done to black Americans is inflicted by those politicians, civil rights leaders and academics who assert that every problem confronting blacks is a result of a legacy of slavery and discrimination. That's a vision that guarantees perpetuity for the problems."

– Walter E. Williams

The fight for equal rights was the fight to be seen as a human-being - as an individual in a society that was attempting to permanently place all black Americans together in one monolithic group. Once a person loses their individuality, it makes it easier for those in power to control a population of people - whether it's through manipulative tactics revolving around race, religion or political ideology. For black Americans, during slavery and the Jim Crow era, all aspects of their life revolved around something they had no control over and were simply born with.

When group discrimination is legalized, those discriminated against wish for the day when they could be seen as an individual not as part of a group. The obvious immorality of judging someone based on outward appearance instead of character was something that black Americans had grown tired of. The ability to create a lower class of citizens and dictate how free they were is an American tragedy. We have no problem today acknowledging how egregious it is to superficially judge others when it is directed at non-white individuals. But we have lost our principals and love weaponizing racism toward a different group now.

We experienced grievances when we were oppressed, but today, we use these same techniques for our benefit. Our fight against racism used to be planned, methodical and with purpose. If we felt wronged in a particular area, we targeted that area with logical measures for change. We were purposeful people with a particular goal that we felt would be satisfactory. But something went awry along the way. We raised our fists in the air as a symbol of black unification, but now this same symbol is used as a threat against the social fabric of America.

With the passage of multiple civil rights laws in the 1960s, we in effect created a new black grievance industry. We learned that we could leverage these legislative wins, along with the guilt of white Americans, to do our bidding. However, the conundrum was that with such a large win, what do we grieve after next? In a changing American landscape that has become less racist with every passing generation, what is there to grieve?

We had a social blind spot resulting from treatment of black Americans that was immoral, unequal and un-American. Once this was realized, white Americans did not want to risk being visually impaired when it came to black strife, so they have now become overly reliant on black grievance as an indicator of reality without understanding that they just allowed a wolf into the henhouse.

The black grievance industry is ruthless and careless in trying to prove that the racist bogeyman of the past has been hiding underneath our beds this whole time. They operate with a "by any means necessary" agenda to convince black Americans that they continue to be wronged and white

Americans that they are still the perpetrators of racial sin. To reach such an achievement, they must embellish or obliterate critical information in an attempt to hide their trickery.

The people that hated being prejudged now use it exclusively for their gain. So, who is actually the oppressor now? We have lied about white men and women based simply on their complexion. We have no problem turning on our cell phone cameras and becoming our own narrator to a fabricated lie because it spreads faster than the truth. We hold no guilt in ruining the livelihoods of innocent people to satisfy our lust for historical revenge.

Our desire to have black leadership has weakened black Americans so we don't realize that the wolf in sheep's clothing is also black. Black leadership's tactics of deception, exaggeration and blatant racism comes at the expense of how black Americans are perceived by everyone else. We are seen as highly emotional, irrational, gullible, incapable of nuance in complex situations, and incapable of shaming criminality from within their own community.

Weaponizing racism against white Americans solves nothing and makes us just as pathetic as the people we despised from our past. Racism is for the simpleton among us who is too shallow to look deeper into someone's character before casting aspersions. Black Americans are not dumb, but we are constantly promoting dumb tactics that feed into our own victimization. We cannot claim to be victims while we oppress, it just does not work that way.

It is obvious that we have taken advantage of the guilt that well intentioned white Americans possess. We have become drunk on the power to manipulate with a simple flash of our black-victim card. This card is essentially a free pass to say whatever we want to white people and if they dare to react, it will be their fault. This card is a free pass to accuse whites of their perceived thoughts without proof, no matter how destructive the aftermath may be.

This card is a recognition that white Americans have no chance in winning the public relations battle. God forbid someone records their altercation with a black person. It does not matter how ignorant, childish, foolish, spiteful or racist we are towards our white counterparts. We will always be perceived as the victim and spoiler alert: we know this.

Take, for example, the altercation between the Atlanta Police Department and Rayshard Brooks. This was a black man who was drunk and asleep behind the wheel, yet when the police officers attempted to punish him for the crime of driving while intoxicated, Rayshard physically assaulted the officers multiple times with strong punches to both of their faces and tackling them to the ground. Rayshard was subsequently shot dead after he stole one of the officer's taser guns and attempted to use it on the officer.

What was the reaction by black Americans to this encounter? It wasn't shunning Rayshard for his criminality and irresponsible behavior. It wasn't recognizing that Rayshard could have fallen asleep while actually driving somewhere and killed someone with his vehicle, which likely in that neighborhood would have been another black person. Unfortunately, our concerns revolved around excoriating the police officers for daring to enforce the law by arresting Rayshard and for attempting to defend themselves while being white.

We don't criticize why he thought it was a good idea to fight the police or why he was even drunk driving in the first place. The only thing that matters is that he was our black brethren, and he was taken by our white oppressor; nothing more. These officers broke the unwritten social agreement that states no white man or woman shall punish, criticize or defend themselves against anyone that is black, and God help you if it gets caught on camera.

The devil we feared is who we have become. We claim we want equality, but if that were true, a phrase like "All Lives Matter" wouldn't hurt our sensibilities. We claim to want black lives to be at the forefront of the discussion to make people aware of a problem but all I can see are the many hands reaching out to grab power by means of social justice activism. Social justice activism has become the buzzword that allows us to dictate discussions, actions and responses to racial grievances. It is also the mechanism that keep blacks as the permanent victim class in America while continuing to leverage white America's guilt. We burn down our own communities and everyone else shrugs their shoulders and talks about how they understand our frustration.

Everyone sees our hunger for power, yet no one addresses it for fear that the starving beast may come after them next. We know the power our words have in claims of racism purely by the imbalance of a white versus black encounter. And we know that everyone will believe us no matter what. With great power comes great responsibility, yet we are irresponsible with how we use it. People like Jussie Smollett used this power to get a nation to weep for him over a fake hate crime. I ask, if there is so much oppression going on, why do we feel the need to make it up? Why do we feel the need to exaggerate?

It's because we know the power we hold in our hands but admitting it would mean giving up our leverage. We are historical victors who could be standing on the shoulders of black giants instead of pretending to be the tragic American black victim. But we have only found power in victimhood. We have given up being morally correct in favor of being morally corrupt. Absolute racial power corrupts absolutely, and no one is willing to call us out, including among ourselves.

The pain of hatred that we wish to avoid is now the pain we are inflicting on everyone else. We hate being discriminated against and yet we do the very same thing when we label others as racist without evidence. It is the social equivalent of sentencing someone to jail for a crime they didn't commit. But with social crimes, there is no unbiased judge, only a self-righteous jury. Unlike a trial jury that is handpicked by both the counsel and defense, the jury of public opinion reaches beyond a single courtroom or city, exaggerates the facts, and is biased and unrelenting.

This jury is multi-cultural yet singularly ready to execute anyone based on a simple accusation. There is a segment of our population that feels powerless in their mundane lives. But with the expansion of social media and the desire for group-think validation, these people relish the opportunity to destroy anyone's social reputation for a simple pat on the back. They project racist assertions into a particular scenario and refuse to consider a viable alternative. These people are indignant about how correct they are without proof and without having reasoned through their conclusions. These people think that they know how to read someone's mind as they poignantly claim to know the intentions of someone they've never met before.

Fighting racism with racism is inexcusable because all it does is create more casualties in this culture war. These casualties are often innocent bystanders who are just trying to live their life. But one accusation can destroy it. In the worst cases, the accusations become publicly known and anyone associated with the accused will have to recant their relationship because they know the power that an accusation of racism currently holds.

No one wants to be seen as a racist or be viewed as supporting a racist, so disassociation is necessary to save one's neck. If you are accused and people believe it, regardless of facts, you risk losing your employment, your home, your relationships and even your freedom. The risk of a racial accusation is so life altering that we now have a population of Americans who are afraid of the slightest misrepresentation of themselves, so they say nothing and do nothing.

Did we really want to create an environment that fears even accidentally offending us? We have people who are too scared to speak openly and critically in fear of black repercussions. Everyone must pretend to agree with our advocacy, even if there are obvious flaws. We now require compliance with our grievances and complete understanding of our demands regardless of rationality. Or else we will mobilize at your expense.

There is no legal recourse for social slander or redemption for the falsely accused. There is rarely a path for forgiveness, and no one ever says "oops, my mistake" after slandering someone's character. How do you prove you are not a racist? Because you have black friends? Well, that's exactly what a racist would say. Because you have a black partner? That's because you fetishize black people. You see where I am going here. There is no suitable answer to give to someone who is aggressive in their determination to classify your intentions as negatively racially motivated. You can plead, apologize or literally bend the knee in a show of solidarity; it will only delay the beating of your character, not prevent it.

In July 2020, there was an incident in Lake Orion Township, Michigan that is a perfect example of the madness that we have created and continually allow. A visibly pregnant white woman, Jillian Wuestenberg, was leaving a Chipotle and was accused of bumping into a black 15-year-old, Makayla Green, as she was exiting. By the time the camera footage starts, all you see is Jillian standing still attempting to explain herself as Makayla and her mother, Takelia Hill, shout her down saying she was disrespectful and that she was, of course, racist simply due to her being white.

Jillian was not combative; she was literally cornered and did not engage them physically even though she was in a vulnerable position. Tensions continued to escalate, and they were preventing Jillian from leaving by impeding her ability to get into her vehicle to escape the situation. That was when Jillian's husband, Eric Wuestenberg, came to her defense to help her leave by assisting her into the passenger side of the vehicle and out of the faces of these angry black females.

A visibly pregnant Jillian slowly gets into the car as these two women are still screaming at her in the process. Takelia shows how much of a masculine black female role model she is by getting in the face of Eric and says, "I'll beat your white ass too. Do something, please put your hands on me!"

"Who the hell do you think you people are? She did nothing to you!" exclaims Eric as he attempts to defend his pregnant wife. The ignorance continues as 15-year-old Makayla verbalizes her accusations "You're very racist and ignorant."

Jillian had enough and rolled down her window to defend herself with such accusations "You can't go around calling white people racist! This is not that type of world!" Eventually Eric had enough of this back and forth and had Jillian roll up the window, but this does not stop the shit talking from both the black females involved. As Eric is attempting to reverse out of the parking spot, Takelia walks into the path of the vehicle that is trying to flee the scene and shouts "You trying to hit me?!" followed by a loud bang due to her hand slamming against the vehicle. This tense scene had now escalated to the point of violence, triggering Jillian to quickly exit the vehicle and pull out her concealed gun while shouting "Get away! Get the fuck away!"

With zero worry in her voice and a gun an arm's reach away, Takelia stands there with her cell phone out recording the encounter. Every time Jillian yells for Takelia to back up, Jillian takes a step back to give separation during this altercation. "Mom! Stop walking!" yells the 15-year-old at her mother. There became a point of a stalemate where Jillian felt safe enough to leave, so she entered her vehicle with her husband and left the scene. The video runs on from the perspective of the 15-year-old crying with the typical accusation of "these white people, they so racist".

The aftermath: Both Jillian and Eric were fired from their jobs almost immediately after this video went viral. Days later, they were charged with assault and are facing years in jail. This entire situation encapsulates so much that is wrong due to the power of racial accusation. It shows the unfortunate black bias that always believes black voices and immediately assumes white guilt. This situation does not differ from any other media driven story that comes out with a black and white encounter because the initial narrative is always based on a lie.

The initial narrative was that a racist white woman pulled a gun on a black family, simply just for existing, and it was backed up by a short out of context video clip that circulated the internet. Within the upcoming days, the full video of the full encounter painted a different picture. It showed on full display the capacity for ignorance that exists in some black people and our capability for sensationalized overreactions to the most minor of situations. The alleged bump may have actually occurred but what they didn't tell you was that this Chipotle only had one door and a large-belly-pregnant Jillian was carrying two large items as she was exiting the store and possibly bumped the 15-year-old due to these circumstances.

Let's assume that she did bump this girl. There was absolutely no reason for this situation to end up where it did. There is no reason for a grown woman to immediately become combative with someone who wasn't attempting to be combative. The obvious reason for this rapid escalation in ignorance is because there is no need to de-escalate when we are always the victim and we know we will be believed, right or wrong.

Takeila and Makayla throughout this entire encounter kept escalating the situation by making threats to both of them while simultaneously referencing Wuestenberg's race. The hypocrisy is that both the mother and the daughter were enraged at even the perception of racism, but they were the only ones being racist. They were the ones who were accusative in this whole situation. They were in the wrong, but we no longer punish the people who are wrong out of fear of social repercussions.

What would have happened if the Sheriff Department charged Takiela for terroristic threats or for hitting the Wuestenbergs vehicle? Well, we know that Al Sharpton's flunkies would have a conniption and trigger the rest of the black grievance industry to raise money for this poor aggrieved black family while protesting for the removal of a racist Sheriff. So instead of doing the right thing at the risk of pissing off a few black people, they charged the white couple because there is no such thing as a white grievance industry.

White people aren't rioting hoping to have all charges dropped for Jillian and Eric. There is no backlash from "White America" because they don't have blind unity like Black America does. Ambiguous situations like this also allow for virtue signaling white people to pile on to show that they are one of the "good white people" in front of a potential black mob that is ready to pounce at any moment. These white people are willing to step on someone else to appease black people, or in other words, sacrifice others to save themselves.

Takeila claimed that these mean angry white people were attempting to hit her with their vehicle but details later emerged that their vehicle has a rear back up motion sensor that prevent their vehicle from hitting anyone or anything by automatically disabling the vehicle which is why in the video they are sitting still after the vehicle was hit by Takeila, making it literally impossible for them to even try to run over Takeila like she claimed.

With an increasingly angry black woman who has now displayed herself as potentially violent by striking her vehicle plus a disabled vehicle, Jillian made the choice to defend herself, her husband and her unborn child. However, Jillian's decision broke one of the agreements of the contract that black and white Americans have signed; you are not allowed to defend yourself against someone that is black, even if it's justified.

I had mentioned Takeila's seeming calmness as a gun pointed in her direction. Takeila understood that she didn't need a gun in retaliation. Her narration of the situation and her black skin is the ultimate weapon. Takeila's calmness represents the knowledge that she will be viewed as the victim, no matter how ignorant, reckless and immature her behavior was.

Takeila was the one who escalated the situation even when the Wuestenbergs were attempting to leave. But this fact is inconvenient. It is well-known that white people, even more so well-intentioned white people, live in fear of social persecution in the absence of facts. The injection of speculation into any situation that involves any self-righteous, entitled and ignorant black person will lead the white person involved into a dead end. I want to make it very clear; this situation would not have happened with a black person who didn't view themself as a victim.

A black person who does not see themself as a victim can think clearly and be objective about any situation. A bump is simply a mistake and you move on. Let's say Jillian was some hardcore racist that intentionally bumped this 15-year-old. A black person without a victim identity probably would have had some words as they were walking to their car to leave. A black person who is not a victim has better things to do in life than fight over something so trivial as being "disrespected".

The people who are so fragile that they are constantly worried about losing the respect of others are the very ones who do not deserve respect anyway. Why would you respect someone like this? Why would you respect a mother who is displaying such unbecoming behavior in front of her child? A mother who is displaying "this is how a woman is supposed to behave" to her own daughter is behaving irredeemably.

Stroll over to YouTube and read some comments about this interaction:

"The black woman was CLEARLY the aggressor here, I don't see what the controversy is about."

"The only racist people were the mother and daughter that happened to be black."

"That young lady is pregnant, seriously? Why even start a fight with a pregnant woman? I love how they turn from aggressors to victims as soon as the steel comes out."

"As a black person. If I was entering a business as someone else is leaving, I believe we both should apologize for a mutual accident. Nevertheless, I definitely would not follow someone to their vehicle using foul, racist, and derogatory remarks. The mother showed a poor display of maturity in front of the children. That was an opportunity to teach how to handle an accident and how to keep a simple situation from escalating."

The comments go on and on from the anonymous public that can see clearly that the black females involved are actually at fault and that they were the aggressors, not the victims in this situation. Publicly, no one of significance will call these black women out simply because they are black. It's just that simple. When we act out publicly, black people won't say "Damn, she was wrong" because it is like insulting a family member. White people won't speak up because they know the beast is always ready for another body to chew up and spit out. In the end, there is no real justice in a world that claims to want social justice.

It is all a show, a facade for the masses, placing importance on feeling righteous instead of being right. Black people hold this social power, and the bad ones leverage it for their own personal satisfaction. Meanwhile the other black people who disagree say absolutely nothing or make excuses for the bad one's ill behavior. The child that is not disciplined grows up to continue to be disrespectful. We neglect to call out our own and we continue to placate niggerish behavior. Americans are content with reactions like Takiela's. Such behavior is viewed as the black cultural standard thus making it acceptable to allow for the public execution of Jillian and Eric.

The old determination of racism was based on actions that were provable and clearly visible. You used to be allowed to apologize for insensitive behavior and move on. Black Americans have an increasing level of power now and can call nearly anything racist. But we still need to have an opposition to fight against. A white person who apologizes is viewed as acknowledging their racism even if they are simply doing it to appease the mob. This never works. And if you attempt to deny your racism, you still lose because you're either a liar or in denial of your own racism.

We have embraced black supremacy in hopes of bringing about some form of black empowerment. But the black empowerment that we are seeking is what is dividing us as Americans. The black empowerment that we claim is necessary for our survival is fueled by victimhood and animosity.

Without a doubt there are people in this world who hate for arbitrary reasons like skin color. However, our counter reaction should not be to hate in the same way they do. Racism is hatred and hatred is part of the human condition. However we should not use tribal markers as our final determination of people's intentions. This determination leads some of us to target those that we feel have wronged us.

For example, in New York City, many of the targeted attacks on Jewish and LGBT residents have been committed by black people. In an article published by the New York Post titled "What the left doesn't want to mention about New York City hate crimes", from 2019, they state the reality of the situation:

"As the investigative reporter -Armin Rosen pointed out in Tablet, "many of the [anti-Jewish] attacks are being carried out by people of color with no ties to the politics of white supremacy." As he noted, even in cases where no one is caught, video footage

overwhelmingly shows minority attackers. Blacks comprised seven of the nine anti-Jewish hate-crime perpetrators arrested during the third quarter.

In the most recent report, blacks comprised 24 of the 34 (71 percent) perpetrators arrested for all hate crimes. After reaching a high of 61 percent in the second quarter of 2018, the black share consistently declined to 14 percent in the second quarter of 2019 but has now shot back up. The NYPD doesn't account for this odd oscillation, though one wonders if there is a political component to this, as well.

Black perpetrators are especially prominent in anti-LGBT crimes, comprising 10 of the 12 arrested for those crimes in the latest quarterly report. Overall, since the beginning of 2017, blacks comprised 56 percent — 61 of 108 — of those -arrested for anti-LGBT hate crimes."

There have been several violent incidents against Asian Americans, especially since the COVID-19 pandemic, and many of them have been committed by black Americans. The Department of Justice Criminal Victimization Statistics, even in 2018, showed that 27.5% of violent crimes against Asians have been committed by black Americans, compared to 24.1% by white Americans. FBI hate crime statistics point out that 23.9% of racially motivated hate crimes were committed by black people, which is disproportionally high compared to the black population.

These statistics and scenarios are uncomfortable, but they are real. I'm not overlooking the statistics of violent crimes against black Americans, I'm well aware of them, but that's not the point of this conversation. We cannot control what other people do, but we can control our own behavior, which will lead to a positive change for the greater black population.

The victim narrative has corrupted our morality, making some of us believe that to not be a victim, you must exert force against others, effectively switching places with your alleged oppressor. When members of the Black Hebrew Israelites, David Anderson and Francine Graham, targeted a Jersey City Jewish market and murdered three people because of their ethnicity, this was a result of black supremacist ideology. This incident of targeted ethnic execution is an extreme example, but it helps to highlight what can happen, and has been happening, when we teeter on the edge of supremacy; sometimes we fall over.

We must strive to hold the moral high ground because hatred only deteriorates our souls. Hatred has made us paranoid and cynical about other racial groups, which is why we are quick to assume that everything is racially motivated. We believe that others' actions are based on race because of our historical oppression, but the truth is that we are holding hatred in our hearts as well.

Resisting hatred is for the strong. Accepting hatred is for the weak. I know there are black men and women of various ages who have experienced racialized hatred, including myself. I remember the first time I was called a nigger. I remember that feeling of being confused and angry as to why my white neighbor called me this heinous word. This experience as a child has been cemented into my brain, not to be turned into hatred but to face the reality of the situation and the world around me.

He was also a child, and children aren't born with hate; they are taught it. I hold no hatred for him because all it would do is tear me apart internally. I hold no hatred because that would leave less room for me to receive love from others and from God.

Many of us are holding onto these experiences of trauma and have been discouraged from seeking forgiveness. We need to let go of these moments and leave them where they happened, in the past. Living your life in fear of something that may never happen to you is quite exhausting. Unrelenting fear of possible racial persecution leaves us on edge, believing that this fateful day will come. What we are ignoring is how this fear makes us act like the very people we are afraid of.

Our black ideologue leaders want us angry because it makes us subservient to their message of victimhood. We are only victims to trauma if we choose to be. If we are carrying this anger around with us daily, it will not only appear when race is an issue, but in every facet of our lives. Anger isn't selective, it's all-encompassing. Once anger permeates your life, embracing the role of the traumatized victim will only further validate your anger. When the life that you wanted doesn't come to fruition, anger will then help you find who to blame. It becomes a vicious cycle.

Many of the black people whom I have met that leaned on these supremacist feelings or had an embedded skepticism of white people, carried so much emotional baggage that it was weighing down their lives. Their lives were miserable because they let others control them. They blamed their shortcomings on someone else taking their opportunities; not admitting that they often gave those opportunities away. The more they leaned into their hatred of others, the more wretched they became.

The promotion of hate within the black community will only produce more unappealing people who walk around this country hoping that someone bumps into them to validate their anger. We are advocating for black people to be hateful social hypocrites toward whites and to play the contradictory roles of victim and supremacist at. We are promoting the confusing message of acting as morally superior racists who are at the same time continual victims. We are also leaving black people across this country stuck reliving their debilitating trauma for the sake of romanticizing the black struggle.

We should strive to improve how we treat each other regardless of race. But expecting the complete abolishment of racism is sadly unrealistic. There will always be hateful people. Letting them control our lives and well-being is killing our optimism and has blinded us to the great number of positive social changes that have occurred with every passing decade. We need optimistic realism to reign in the black community rather than being stuck demanding the impossible.

– CHAPTER 9 –

SAVIORS AND VICTIMS

"Half of the harm that is done in this world is due to people who want to feel important. They don't mean to do harm. But the harm does not interest them."

—T.S. Eliot
"The Cocktail Party"
(1949),
Act 1,
Scene 1.

In October 2018, I had the opportunity to take a multi-city solo trip around Europe. I was in the midst of a personal transformation for betterment and wanted to experience other cultures firsthand. On this list would be a new country, Portugal. I purposefully didn't research the city so I could take in the cultural shock of being somewhere that differed vastly from the northeast of the United States. Landing in the city of Lisbon was an amazing experience, and tourism was booming. During multiple tours, I met other Europeans who were also on vacation or temporarily living in Lisbon for their education.

One of my favorite pastimes as I traveled was talking about American politics with people not from America. I found quickly that everyone knows what is going on in America, but there would always be questions as to why we have certain policies in place that are vastly different from other western countries. For example, I was in London during the Las Vegas mass shooting and a couple of Australians questioned why we are obsessed with guns. They had removed guns from their society after one mass shooting.

One day while in Lisbon, I was gallivanting with two French women who I met the previous day on a walking tour. Late in the afternoon we decided to stop for lunch at a packed sushi restaurant in a heavy tourist district. When you're in a high tourist area, you don't know where anyone is from just by looking at them. As a foreigner, I took this opportunity to speak more openly about topics that may be seen as controversial such as political discussion.

The two French women I was with asked me questions about different political topics and I would explain why we did things in a particular way in the U.S - of course, in my opinion. Looking back at this experience, I believe most of what I said was incredibly left leaning and my diligence in considering other perspectives was lacking. Nevertheless, I preached openly about my views on American politics.

Suddenly, I heard someone say, "Excuse me". It was an older white woman who was sitting next to us. She wanted to compliment me. To paraphrase, "You are so young and so wise to understand what is going on in American politics". Come to find out, she was also an American who was a retired doctor living in Mexico and was a like-minded leftist. She proceeded to co-sign my rhetoric, and I listened to her perspective as well. For what it was worth, it was a nice cordial conversation.

Then the topic switched to race. In my conversation with the French women, we had not brought up the topic of race. But this older leftist woman decided to. She proceeded to say something that I thought was shockingly audacious. I will never forget her words: "Republicans don't see you as anything else but a nigger".

I am not typically someone that holds onto the "White people can't say the n-word". However, white Americans of all political spectrums understand there is a level of sensitivity when it comes to this word, justified or unjustified. There is an unspoken rule of "If you're not black, just don't say it" as a safety measure so that you do not personally offend or in the worst case, get assaulted. We all know this, including this mystery left-leaning white woman. To place it more into focus, I was a stranger to her, yet she felt comfortable using this word in my presence with her skin tone. She had no idea of the level of sensitivity I had to this word, and lucky for her, I do not have much of a sensitivity to it because I am not a nigger.

This leftist white woman had no hesitancy about saying what she said. Just because we are in another country does not mean the rules change when it is an American-to-American interaction. She felt comfortable saying what she said because she thought the word "nigger" was simply a quote from those on the right side of the political aisle, but it was in fact her word. She had zero problems invoking race or racism in my presence, even when that was not the topic at hand. Even worse, she had no problem invoking the prospect of political racism toward someone like me.

This woman is just one person. However, it has become a trend to invoke racial victimhood as a form of kinship between different races of the same political spectrum. White leftists have become oh so comfortable throwing around racist words and statements because they feel that they have a "black pass" due to them thinking that we are of the same political mindset. White leftists in particular have invoked claims of racism against blacks as a smear tactic against their opposition on the right because it is unprovable either way. Claims of racism are made to insult those on the other side of the political aisle, and this is callously done at the expense of black people.

How are white leftists able to get away with constantly using black people as their political weapon? Simple, we allow it. We have invited victimhood into our homes for generations and fed it every day to avoid looking at our own individual and communal responsibilities. If you are a victim, you are not accountable for the downfalls and degradation you experience. It must be the racist white people who manipulated our feeble black brains into living in American slums with low expectations. It is a "woe is me" mindset held by people whom I believe are just as capable as anyone else.

Continual victimhood, encouraged and maintained by those on the left, is the mental slavery that we volunteered for because of our sensitivity to the historical wrongs we experienced. These are the people that are constantly bringing up slavery as if it were a couple of years ago because they want you to remember that you are still a victim. Those African slaves of the past were kidnapped and trafficked into Western society to do the bidding of white people. Those on the left want you to understand that this can happen again. This is not a warning, but a threat.

A victim attitude has been and always will be stronger than any chain someone can put black people into. A chained man with hope will fight for his freedom, a victimized man will give up even without being restrained.

Black people use victim phraseology like "You have to work twice as hard to get half as far" or "You are born with two strikes before you come to the plate" as a constant mental reminder that you are a victim and it's the

144

fault of someone else if you don't succeed - mainly white people. Victimized black leftists claim there is a boot on black peoples' necks, but we own a pair of those boots too. Once you remove the boot from your neck, the victimized black person next to you will question how you were able to do so because they are unable to see the skin color of the foot in those boots.

Black people have to work twice as hard to fight the normalcy of hand out culture so they can have true independence. Black people have to work twice as hard to remove mental victimhood because it has been reinforced by public school education. Black people have to work twice as hard to see past the leftist media's profit machine that makes sure we live in fear of the police. Yes, black people have to work twice as hard to be accurately informed about the world around us as it is easier to stay in a coma than it is to wake up from it.

I agree that black people are born with two strikes in America. Strike one is fatherlessness and strike two is leftist ideology. Fatherlessness leaves you vulnerable to the allure of victim ideologies because a real father would never let their child victimize themselves. Leftist ideology constantly reinforces your victimhood, dependency and desire for acceptance and approval. Statements like "Black Lives Matter" are unnecessary to a conservative because they are obvious. Statements like "Black Lives Matter" are necessary to a leftist because victims always need an advocate, and the leftist wants to play that rescuing role.

One can be financially lacking and not mentally impoverished, much like one may have been a victim and yet not carry a victim mentality. Black people of yesteryear have legitimate grievances due to governmental oppression, however, this does not entitle modern day blacks to remain mentally victimized.

Imagine a woman who was physically assaulted by her husband for years speaking with her psychologist. She describes tales of narrowly escaping death and how this has left her feeling scared to be around men. What if the psychologist said, "Men are dangerous, never to be trusted, and you should never forget what he did to you because the abuse you experienced is what you will constantly experience from men"? We would collectively gasp at this horrendous generalization of men as abusers and call out the psychologist for allowing her patient to remain victimized due to this over-generalization.

For the sake of this analogy, black Americans are the abused woman and the leftists among us are the psychologist committing malpractice. We are always being reminded of our historical pain because we are viewed as nothing but victims to the modern-day leftist. They are always implying that we need their help to achieve and, God forbid, one of us pulls ourselves up from mediocrity! We would be viewed as the exception not the rule. The constant effort to keep black Americans as the perpetual victim-class doesn't benefit the black community - but only the leftists who encourage it. Whether it be to achieve financial gain, political gain or simply to think they are doing something positive, their actions promote them into an elevated status as the new savior class.

THE NEW LEFTIST SAVIOR CLASS

"I can deal with an honest bigot more than a patronizing leftist. I can change a bigot faster than I can a patronizing liberal." – Robert L. Woodson Sr. / "Uncle Tom Documentary"

It is only natural to feel sorry for someone who is a victim. When you see someone victimized by fraud for example, you intrinsically feel bad, and you want to help by giving them advice or crowdsourcing the money that they lost. However, this empathy can easily turn into pity for the victimized - in this case, the victimized black. Once you begin to pity someone, you begin to doubt that they are capable of returning to a position of strength and independence. The pitied can become reliant on this pity. Mutual respect dwindles away, leaving nothing, but a relationship built on subservience in which both parties silently agree on the new terms of their interaction.

There is a new leftist savior class that has a need to express their superiority and pity amongst those that they deem less fortunate. You could possibly label it as guilt of privilege or the need to declare how good of a citizen they are. Even if their intentions may be good, their results are destructive to black Americans.

The new leftist savior class has made pet projects out of black Americans' plight by promoting causes that do nothing to actually help black people but which they state are on behalf of black people. They utilize social media to display how "woke" they are but remain asleep to how unhelpful their superficial advocacy actually is. They gesture to anyone willing to watch how morally correct they are by helping the unfortunate Negroes among them by sending a hashtag or by changing their profile picture to a black box. Sadly, by today's standards, these actions are the equivalent to marching from Selma to Montgomery.

The new leftist savior class sacrifices nothing of importance when they engage in their advocacy. But they gladly accept all the adulation that comes with virtue signaling to their fellow leftists. Their view of black America is one of unremarkable people who need to be saved from themselves. Black America, from the perspective of the new savior class, is incapable of being capable.

The most awake white leftist will be outwardly masochistic about their race's wrongdoings while simultaneously signaling their superiority by recommending that only they are capable of saving black America from itself. This individual is likely of a higher class but likes to categorize themselves as equal with those who are actually suffering, all for the sake of receiving the highly coveted victim points.

The new savior class wants to reassure black America that they will do whatever it takes to help, as long as you stay in a position of needing help. The new savior class is not about uplifting others but uplifting themselves for social currency. Understand that all of this alleged saving is superficial nonsense. Black Americans do not need anyone but themselves. Black people are more than capable of striving for what they need, even through seemingly impossible odds.

Black history is not the history of victims, it is the history of overcomers. True black history displays how we fought to change a system that was legalizing inequality while keeping our community intact and contributing to American society. The black history that we are not told about consists of our contributions to America outside of servitude. The painting of black history as people sitting idly by waiting for white people to give us a voice to express our grievances is an incorrect portrait.

For example, Garrett Morgan, a black businessman and inventor, patented the first gas mask in 1912, which was subsequently used during World War I and helped firefighters of his time. Who knows how many lives this man saved in America and throughout the world because of his invention? This was a man who did not wallow in victimhood, even when he could have easily embraced it. This was a man who was born 12 years after the abolishment of slavery, yet he became something that we could all aspire to. There is a long list of black people throughout history that overcame incredible odds to contribute to this world. So why do we need help now?

The key word is "need". The lie that the new liberal savior class wants black Americans to believe is that without them we cannot achieve success. There is no other racial minority in America that this attitude is directed towards except for the black population.

If you want to know how to spot someone who fits this new savior class, look at their actionable advocacy because they likely lack in this department. The new savior class wants platitudes and not actual change. Positive change in black America would remove them from the equation. So, they will make sure to misdirect where we actually need assistance so we can keep chasing our tails. They will hyper focus on police brutality but will shy away from talking about black-on-black brutality. They will excuse single parenthood as an empowering trend while our children look on helplessly wondering where their other half is. They will advocate for the indiscriminate release of jailed black individuals, no matter their history of terrorism within their respective black communities.

These people are not heroes, they are narcissists. Their life mission is to chase applause, hoping they end up on the right side of history. These are the vain people who will march alongside black people for an hour so they can get more "likes" on social media. These are also the same people that steal from a black owned business in a black neighborhood, all for so-called justice.

When a black neighborhood burns and ashes fall upon the feet of the new savior class, they will gleefully cheer on our destruction. Their misguided ideology says that destruction of black property is freedom, while the incorporation of black businesses is the markings of white colonialism being forced upon these unfortunate victims. God forbid there is a business within these neighborhoods that is not owned by someone with the same complexion as its patrons. They will garner even less empathy as their business goes up in flame.

They will legitimize their actions by saying "they weren't black owned" while overlooking the fact that they were black serving. Black people used and needed their services, like a corner store that sells small grocery items in a food desert. Consider the hypocrisy of these people: they are not checking the complexion of the store owners in their middle- or upper-class white majority neighborhoods. The new savior class enforces "racial rules for thee, not for me."

The new savior class is hypocritical because their ideological dogma is inconsistent. Stereotyping is considered racist, but all they do is stereotype. They think that all black people want the same things or think the same things. So how does someone like me fit into their equation? Their brains scramble when they come across a victimless black American, but eventually they will be sure to mark them as a sympathizer of their white oppressor to keep feeling sorry for them. The new savior class pities a victimless black because from their perspective, these Negroes simply just do not know what is good for them.

"I can't believe you can't see how racist America is…"

This is a quote from a former friend from Europe who had the audacity to declare to me, a black American, what America is when he's never lived in this country and is also not black. Although I disagree with many viewpoints of other black people in America, I understand how they have come to their conclusions based on their personal experiences. What audacity this European had to tell a grown black man how he should feel, think and react to a society that he is not associated with and has zero experience living.

Our friendship slowly fell apart after this because he was unwilling to allow me to be a free-thinking black man rather than living like a victim searching for a savior. In multiple conversations, he referred to his advocacy as his attempts to "save me" when no one asked him for his help. He had no interest in understanding that the more I pulled away from believing I'm a helpless victim, the happier I've been able to live my life. He didn't want to hear about my personal experiences of feeling helpless to anxiety or shaking when I've been pulled over by a cop because of the victim narrative forced down black American's throats. He especially didn't want to congratulate me for overcoming my fears and finding a way to empower myself.

His idea of what black is revolves around what he sees on television. But when he has a living, breathing black American in front of him, he would prefer to lean on his preconceived notions rather than hearing what I have to say. He's the type of person that feels he understands what it means to be black because he went to a hip-hop club once. He's the type of person that says we should listen to black voices but easily disregards my voice.

My voice as a victor is not suitable to those with a savior complex. From his perspective, I was performing wrong-think and for such a crime, I should be re-educated to behave according to his ideas of how a black American should behave. He would prefer me saying that I live in fear of dying by the hands of white people rather than me stating that I am the master of my own destiny.

He is the type of person who thinks that he is making some type of noble declaration because he posted on social media that he has "White

Privilege" and can't for a second understand how condescending that statement is to black people. By stating that you have privilege, you are saying that you have some sort of power while simultaneously stating that only whites have this illustrious power. If this is the case, that means that they believe that no black person can be powerful or capable within their society. If I am without power, then I must live my life in hopes that they are gracious enough to bend over, look down upon me and hand me a piece of their privilege.

"Don't you know that you're oppressed?" Translation: You are too dumb to know what is good for you. The only people that are attempting to oppress people like me are these self-appointed saviors. The reality is that they pretend to be fighting against racism. But they are demonstrating racist ideas when they believe that the black man's issues are centered around the level of white generosity that is present. This ideology strengthens the argument that we are the white man's burden. The white guilt that a white leftist may feel is projected onto everyone else because if they feel this way about black people, everyone else must as well. To relieve their guilt, they must overcompensate by saving us from ourselves.

What my former friend failed to understand was that I would rather be called a nigger than be treated like one. His rhetoric of needing to save me is the equivalent of treating me like a nigger who is too ignorant to do for himself. Are you one of these people who act as pseudo-activists by tweeting black activism hashtags and blacking out your profile picture in hopes of saving someone like me? What you're actually doing is using technology to reinforce our status as society's niggers while we are trying to escape that oppressive label.

The truth is that victims need saviors and saviors need victims. Victims need someone to blame for their misfortune. Saviors need a victim to maintain their delusions of grandeur. With the proliferation of social media, companies have commoditized narcissism and promoted false self-importance to mask true insecurity. While black Americans romanticize struggle, our new saviors romanticize empathy. Even if they genuinely want to help, they lack the awareness to understand when they need to stop helping us.

Victims don't know how to be accountable for their actions, and saviors refuse to make victims responsible for their portion of the struggle. Helplessness is the currency that victims are given by their newfound saviors on a daily basis, and there is a never-ending supply of it in America.

We got to the current racial situation in America because we found a way to profit from the pain of black history, generating billions in the process. We made it to this point because we would rather give a slanted historical perspective, making white people our only oppressors, while ignoring the African kingdoms that captured us and sold us in the first place. We made it to this place because of the purposeful overlooking of American history in which blacks chose not to be victims even when they would have had every excuse.

They may be saviors, but they are only interested in saving themselves. Our leftist saviors have no problem putting on "pussy hats" to advocate for the death of black unborn children. Our leftist saviors shrug their shoulders when black men are gunned down senselessly every year, thousands at a time, by someone that looks like me. Our leftist saviors have no problem pushing for affirmative action for black college students but are nowhere to be found when they are mismatched into colleges in which they inevitably fail. The more they attempt to save us, the more they are oppressing us.

There needs to be a conscious pushback against this mindset that is running rampant throughout the Western World. We need to stop accepting apologies while those who are apologizing keep their boots on our necks. Black Americans are more than capable of saving themselves individually first and within our community second. There needs to be an understanding that our suffering is necessary to grow from it, but "our saviors" keep interfering by giving us handouts and platitudes.

They want a "thank you", but they deserve a "fuck you" for interfering with our prosperity. I refuse to thank someone who advocates for my dependency on another man or government as a means for my success. These saviors need us more than we need them, and the sooner we reject their proposition, the quicker we can start to think for ourselves. There are plenty of solutions that can help black Americans, that don't involve the employment of neo-narcissists or collusion with the government.

Black Americans historical strength has always been in our resilience and once this is realized, we will no longer need these pretend messiahs. We will no longer be swayed by their empathy because we do not need it. We will no longer accept the excuses they allow us for things that we should not be excusing. We will no longer need these racial ideologues to dictate our individual wants so they can be selfishly rewarded. Their false advocacy is the poison in black Americans' wells, and we've been drinking from it for way too long.

- CHAPTER 10 -

THE MISEDUCATION AND MISUNDERSTANDING OF BLACK CONSERVATIVES

"My friends, all I'm trying to say is that if we are to go forward today, we've got to go back and rediscover some mighty precious values that we've left behind. That's the only way that we would be able to make of our world a better world, and to make of this world what God wants it to be and the real purpose and meaning of it. The only way we can do it is to go back and rediscover some mighty precious values that we've left behind."

—Martin Luther King Jr.
Sermon in Detroit,
Michigan
1954.

In order to stay principled in my criticisms of black culture throughout this book, I have to be critical of myself as well. Conservatism, personally, felt like a dirty word. It seemed like a word meaning selfish, compassionless concepts and one rooted in racism. The idea of black conservatism seemed like an oxymoron because I viewed conservatism as being at odds with the needs of black Americans. Due to this apparent contradiction, I wondered how someone could be black and conservative? I have since learned that we are purposely mis-educated about what conservatism is and the role of conservatism within black America.

Regardless of race, conservatism is about personal values and embracing individualism. Conservatism is about appreciating how self-determination can enable us to improve ourselves instead of being handed opportunities that were undeserved or given out of pity. Conservatives see individualism as a way for each of us to live as freely as possible and not be enslaved to the narrative of the collective. If individualism is the philosophy that one believes in, then race is not nearly as important. Race is used as an identifier for the collective, not the individual.

The difference between individualism and collectivism when discussing race is simple: collectivism says that I am a black man, individualism says that I am a man who happens to be black. The difference is significant when discussing the topic of race because it determines how you view people and how you treat them.

People base their views on their life interactions. We have to actively fight the impulse to not group people together, especially if you have a negative experience with a member of a particular group. With collectivism, someone like me has to pay for the sins of those that I don't even know purely because we have a similar origin story or skin tone. Judgment by collectivists, whether it is positive or negative, is based on features that I was born with and had no control over.

Individualism sees me for who I truly am and allows me to express myself in any manner that I choose. Individualism is freeing because it allows for me to not be boxed in with the collective in thought and actions. Individualism is freedom, freedom is choice, and together it is the choice to be a free individual. Conceptually, a conservative who is strong in their belief in individualism, has a moral conflict if they are trying to judge me by my race and not by my character. This contradiction is hard to live by, which is why I would argue that conservatives tend to be some of the least racist people due to their lack of desire to judge based on the actions of others or on preconceived notions.

If this is the case, why is racism or race in general always mentioned when talking about conservatives? Simple, it is a mechanism of control and behavioral manipulation. The fact that racism is so demonized in America means it is simply not acceptable. Calling someone a racist in 1920 probably didn't have the same sting as it does today. This unacceptance is a positive in our country, but there are those who have found a way to weaponize racism and benefit politically as they watch their opponents attempt to disprove an unprovable slanderous claim.

How do you prove someone is racist? Maybe you could tell by the words that they use. For example, if someone calls me a nigger, I have a legitimate claim. However, today, we live in a world that claims that people speak in deceptive coded language called "dog whistles." Dog whistling is supposed to imply that the person talking is speaking in a coded language that only their followers understand. But the person who is telling you it is a dog whistle always seems to understand. Not much of a dog whistle in my opinion. More accurately, it is bullshit.

Racism in politics is a tool to oppress through manipulation and by creating a call to action against one's adversaries. Politicians attack conservatism so that their constituents will attack conservatives. Politicians, with the assistance of the mainstream media, create the narrative that race or racism is the motivating factor behind the opposition. If conservatives don't like something, those on the left will tie it to a possible racial dynamic so that it can be used to cause a political reaction. For example, conservatives tend to not be fans of the current welfare system, so this dislike is weaponized by the opposition, conjuring up the stereotype of black people on welfare, concluding that this is a dog whistle for their hatred against blacks.

Never mind that conservatives typically don't like the welfare system because they feel it creates a dependency on the government, regardless of race, while making the government stronger and the individual weaker. This narrative has been repeatedly projected onto conservatives without their consent. Those who hold the microphone control the narrative and the ideas of conservatism are being vilified by those on the left.

When I was in my mid-20s, I became interested in politics. I was explicitly told that the Democrats are the party for black people and that Republicans were racists. Naively, I followed this train of thought for years, believing that I was on the side of righteousness in the battle against racists. I had contempt for conservatives because I had become indoctrinated by my new leftist tribe. Everything was presented to me through the prism of race, and my blackness was seemingly constantly under attack by conservatives, or so said the media. If there was an angle to be taken advantage of, that could create some racial motive on behalf of conservatives or Republicans, the media was sure to expose it.

When I would see a black conservative on television, it was always through clips and not long form discussion about their viewpoints. Snippets of information were manipulated to create a narrative that could only muster disgust from the black ideologues on the political left. There were no qualms about insinuating that their conservative policy position was due to their hatred of black people despite them having black skin. You can publicly call a black conservative anything you want without repercussions. They are the punching bag for your racial animosity and the monster that hides in your black children's closet. On mainstream television, you can call them Uncle Toms, Sell-Outs, or whatever disparaging racial insult that you can hurl to fracture the perception of their intelligence and intentions.

Although I refrained from using these words because those same words had been used against me for arbitrary reasons throughout my life, I still looked at black conservatives with suspicion, as if they were chameleons trying to infiltrate black society. I viewed them like Carlton from The Fresh Prince of Bel-Air - as black men who dressed in suits and spoke with a high pitch voice to impress white America by criticizing black America. They were always portrayed as imposters who were speaking against black people to tear them down. They were never viewed as desiring change for the betterment of black people. For these traitors, there was no benefit of the doubt given and they were easily dismissed. This is unfortunately the mindset that I used to subscribe to.

Our miseducation about conservatism is a purposeful attempt to misinform black Americans so that we will reject the value system that gave us strength decades ago. In the past we rejected handout-culture in pursuit of personal achievement through hard work. We valued our strong family bond with a traditional nuclear family, and this bond was solidified by our love for God. We were without a doubt living life as social conservatives, exemplifying the moral values that Martin Luther King Jr. consistently preached.

"My friends, all I'm trying to say is that if we are to go forward today, we've got to go back and rediscover some mighty precious values that we've left behind."

The values that Martin Luther King Jr. is referring to, in my opinion, are our moral values and our principles. Our moral values within the black community have been tainted, and now we place more value in whether one is righteously black than righteous in God's eyes. We wear our love for blackness to cast hatred upon those that are white. Today, the group of people that see something is wrong within the black community are the black conservatives who are treated with such contempt.

It's alright to lie about the intentions of black conservatives as long as you do it with dignity, right? It's alright to smear and degrade black men and women as being traitorous when they are abiding by God's moral law instead of political tribalism. It's alright to use extortion as a means to silence their dissenting viewpoints as long as it satisfies the black ideologues. Dr. King's description of the direction that black Americans were heading was the flashing yellow traffic light warning us of an impending detrimental shift in our culture and we drove right through it.

Black conservatives want a resurrection of morality and principles to rid our souls of white animosity and black supremacy. The criticisms expressed by black conservatives are not meant to pass judgment on black Americans but to prevent them from receiving negative judgment in God's eyes. We have encouraged morally corrupt behavior like abortion to satisfy political tribalism. We have embraced the few that act devilishly violent and without regard for human suffering as part of black culture. We may say that we are all children of God, but our actions indicate otherwise.

Let us not be confused, this is not some sort of savior complex. We are well aware that we are all flawed children of God. Our advocacy comes from a place of good intention and with a message that can help bring awareness to how we've been steered away from true moral virtue. There are people who are actively attempting to keep us focused on trivial situations for political gain while alluding to our presumed hatred by American society instead of focusing on our known love from God.

"Who shall separate us from the love of Christ? Shall tribulation, or distress, or persecution, or famine, or nakedness, or danger, or sword? As it is written, 'For your sake we are being killed all the day long; we are regarded as sheep to be slaughtered.' No, in all these things we are more than conquerors through him who loved us. For I am sure that neither death nor life, nor angels nor rulers, nor things present nor things to come, nor powers, nor height nor depth, nor anything else in all creation, will be able to separate us from the love of God in Christ Jesus our Lord." – Romans 8:35-39

We have to ask ourselves why there is such hatred against black conservatives or black republicans in the political realm? Why is there no benefit of the doubt given that they actually care about black people? How come white people are allowed to have varying viewpoints that don't generate such traitorous disgust? It is a visceral disgust that can be seen on someone's face when presented with a black person who is interpreted as a living contradiction. They are treated as the social pariahs of mainstream black culture and they must be referred to as dissidents regardless of the fact that they possess the right skin because they have the wrong mind.

"I think Justice Thomas on the United States Supreme Court is an Uncle Tom. A black man allowed himself to be used to carry the message of a white man, which is against the interests of black people in America. In my opinion, that's an Uncle Tom. In my opinion, Clarence Thomas is a very prolific Uncle Tom." – Alabama State Representative Alvin Holmes (Democrat)

"Ben Carson is a 21st Century Uncle Tom" – Headline from the publication Affinity Magazine.

"Carson's actions have prompted many, including myself, to label him as an Uncle Tom. But we might be wrong about that: "Uncle Tom" may be too good of a title for the HUD secretary." – Article published by Salon titled "Ben Carson's infinite fall from grace."

"Martin Luther King is just a 20th century or modern Uncle Tom or a religious Uncle Tom who was doing the same thing today to keep Negroes defenseless" – Malcolm X

"Black Trump supporters refuse to reconcile with the ignorant anti-blackness he's been spouting and have decided to rally behind the idea that they are 'free thinkers.' They parrot alt-right talking points like it's some form of independent thought. We call it 'cooning.'" – Pastor Talbert Swan

"This coon…" – Richwood, LA Mayor Gerald Brown in response to a picture of Candace Owens

"Do any of you guys trust Uncle Clarence…" – MSNBC's Joy Reid

"We've all known [Sheriff David Clarke] to be crazy and he's an Uncle Tom" - SiriusXM satellite radio's Mark Thompson commenting live on MSNBC

"Uncle Tom. Step & fetch Negro. The end." – CNN pundit Sophia A. Nelson commenting about Kentucky Attorney General Daniel Cameron

These comments were made by black people and levied against black conservatives publicly. Some of these statements were made on live television with little to no pushback. No black person loses their job, credibility or sponsorships when they attack black conservatives with racially traitorous language. There is also no questioning why they are attacking the validity of their blackness when it is simply a political disagreement. The leftist political establishment is perfectly fine with black-on-black political aggression and even at times allows for white leftists to question the blackness of black conservatives when they publicly ask if they are "truly black".

Blacks calling other blacks Uncle Toms, Coons, Oreos is nothing new and has been in the black lexicon for decades. These terms have become normalized rhetoric in the political realm as well. Culture trickles downward into politics and in this case, black culture has trickled downward into black politics. Black Americans are nearly politically monolithic, as we are largely Democrats. Black culture has taught us that we must "always stick with our own" and "never turn your back on your people", which are phrases that you would express to someone to prevent them from being viewed as a traitor.

With our growing membership in the cult of blackness and increasing interest in the political world after the civil rights era, we have created a new enemy. This enemy knows the weakness of the cult, making the structure of the cult vulnerable to their criticisms and division. It is either kill or be killed. Or in the case of black politics, defame or be defamed.

The black elite understand that the lower-level members of the cult will cling onto the ideology of blackness, making it easier for the elite to control black people and conquer their will. The black elite understand that you must give someone something to fight against to keep them distracted from seeing what is actually happening behind the curtain. They also understand that you can create paranoia by stating that the enemy is within, making everyone question each other and need to prove their loyalty to the cult. This leads to the question of whether someone is indeed black enough.

If black public figures like mayors, television hosts and writers can use racial assassination with impunity, what makes us think that this will not be seen as perfectly acceptable in a private interaction? The fact is that it does happen, and the pressure is always present for you to either conform or keep your thoughts to yourself to prevent ostracization.

Black Americans have been thoroughly misled about black conservatives. The fact that I have to reference them with racial indicators means that we default black people as someone that is not having conservative thoughts.

Conservatives who happen to be black are not traitors or people that hate their skin. This claim is derogatory nonsense. You are truthfully critical of the people that you love. You judge those that you hate. When conservatives talk about the black illegitimacy rate, it's not to scold black people. It's to wake them up to a growing problem. When conservatives minimize claims of racial bias, it's not because we don't care, but to keep us focused on more imperative issues that we are able to control. When conservatives don't obsess over a police incident involving a black death, it's not because we are okay with black people dying. On the contrary, it is because we understand the rarity of these situations statistically and they don't measure up to the thousands of black bodies that lie dead in the streets each year by our own hands.

It took me decades to realize these aspects of conservatism and how I was indoctrinated to despise these people based on false notions. I never grew up around conservatives, and yet I irrationally disliked them. If I'm honest, I only knew of a few open Republicans of any race in my life, and I never took the time to even discuss their point of view. One of the changing points in my life was when I was traveling abroad and connected with a man originally from England who was living in Madrid by the name of Louis Leseur.

We connected on a human level and based on our interest in football (soccer). We met by coincidence in an Irish pub in Madrid. When I was heading home for the evening God rained down on the city as if he were telling me to stay put. With no umbrella and more games coming on television, I stayed and chatted him up along with his female companion. Even though we were from different parts of the world, we had a lot in common and his genuineness was something that helped spark our long-distance friendship. Our conversations over time went from just talking about sports to diving into culture and politics. This is when I found out that he held conservative views.

As I spoke with him, I realized that maybe I was wrong and maybe I had been manipulated into believing conservatives disliked me for attributes that I could not control. He genuinely respected me, and the feeling was mutual. For the first time in my life, I listened to a conservative without preconceived hatred on my part. In Matrix terms, he was my Morpheus, and I took the red pill.

It took me traveling thousands of miles away and befriending a British conservative to actually feel comfortable enough to listen to conservative values. He introduced me to Thomas Sowell, a prolific author and senior fellow at Stanford University's Hoover Institution, as well as other prominent conservative names. Traveling down the rabbit hole led me to other extremely intelligent conservative thinkers like Walter E. Williams and Shelby Steele. These were deep thinking men who made me question my biases, my indoctrination, and my values.

I realized that my values were no different from conservative values. But I wasn't living my life based on these principles because leftist ideas were so much more flexible. I was practicing what I would call selective principles, basically being principled when it was convenient for the argument or policy that my leftist tribe wanted. I also realized how much I enjoyed listening to factual information rather than the emotional reactionary thinking that is promoted by leftists. The more information that I consumed about conservatism and the more conversations I had with conservatives, the more I agreed with them.

The "red pill" that allowed me to explore conservatism didn't convert my personal and political ideology per se. Instead, it woke me up to the fact that I was already a conservative who was masquerading as a leftist for the purpose of racial and political assimilation. I realized that I had been pushed in a direction that I disagreed with and that ultimately produced results that have been detrimental morally and politically for the black community.

These realizations led me to acknowledge that I had spent years of my life being part of the problem and not the solution. I had discarded the achievements of great men and women, all because they were on the other side. Dr. Ben Carson went from poverty to being one of the best neurosurgeons in the world. Clarence Thomas went from poverty to the Supreme Court. Carol Swain, a child of a third-grade dropout and a high school dropout herself, was able to reinvent herself and earn a PhD in political science which would later allow her to teach at Princeton University and Vanderbilt University.

I encourage you to look into their life stories and understand what they went through. Some of them experienced blatant racism and other obstacles before reaching success. These are people who leaned on their individualism to strengthen themselves and surpass what others expected of them. They also had faith in God, knowing that he would help to guide them in the direction of prosperity. They did not give in to the negativity which encourages us to focus on why we can't achieve our goals.

"My mother told me if I work hard and I really believed in American principles and I believed in God, anything is possible. That's why I'm not anxious to give away American values and principles for the sake of political correctness." – Dr. Ben Carson

We have lost sight of our true individual selves to satisfy the collective. But no one will advocate more for you than yourself. Individualism is freedom. Individualism allows you to be free to succeed or fail as much as you want and as often as you want. Individualism is healthy selfishness. One must help themself before they can help others. Individualism is equality because it allows everyone to choose for themselves how they want their life to turn out. But it cannot guarantee equal outcomes. Nothing can.

"But let each one test his own work, and then his reason to boast will be in himself alone and not in his neighbor." – Galatians 6:4

Conservatives believe in individualism because human history has shown the horrors that result when too much power is given to those in charge. Power is intoxicating, and if the collective is persuaded by those who seek power, then the collective becomes vulnerable to do the bidding of the corrupt. Individualism is the decentralization of power which helps to prevent moral corruption.

Black Americans have been pushed into believing in the wonders of racial collectivism. But the black collective as a concept is deceptive. The collective does not decide what it needs. The few at the top do. You can tweet and post about your trivial wants, but the leaders of the collective are actually steering the ship. As I grew in my understanding of the benefits of individualism, the collectivist attempts to steer me into the path of victimhood, pity and racial paranoia did not work anymore because God had helped me to lift the veil and see the deception.

Collectivism is what led to post-Slavery Jim Crow laws, explicitly to oppress black Americans. These were governmental laws that helped to maintain white preservation, regardless of its impact on others. The leaders of the collective always want more power and they will try to find a way to utilize the might of the government for means of oppression, not goodwill.

Conservatives understand this potential danger, which is one of the reasons why we advocate for a smaller government. We understand that the more money the government has by means of taxes, the greater the potential for corruption and oppression. If you want to be angry at something, don't be angry with a specific group of people. Be angry at collectivism and how collectivists have consistently used the government to impede the lives of black Americans.

Our ancestors fought against those who used their collective power against us. The civil rights fight was an effort to fight the collectivists in government who were using laws to restrict black Americans' liberty and individuality. The collectivists wanted black Americans to see themselves as pseudo-Americans by reminding them constantly that they were different - they were colored. Today, many of us are living our lives based on what the collectivists of the past wanted. We label ourselves with a hyphenated, barely American status: African-American.

Why must black people hyphenate their nationality to be correct politically? Our ancestry goes deeper into this country than most other Americans. I don't believe that our brave ancestors died in wars and made tremendous sacrifices just to be called Africans all over again. The wrongs of the past were not simply that blacks were treated improperly, it was that the government did not live up to the principles of its founding. Conservatives understand that even if our branches have become rotten at various points in our country's history, the roots of our country's tree are solid.

Decreasing collectivism within black culture would not mean that black culture disappears. It would mean a more expansive culture that isn't dependent on a singular monolithic perspective. Every culture has a variety of subcultures within it. Embracing individualism would allow black culture to become more inclusive of people who vary in perspective and expression. It would be a culture that cherishes diversity of thought and removes the cult-like mentality.

Social conservatism is thoroughly misunderstood by many Americans because it is purposely misrepresented by those who oppose it. This misrepresentation is even more pronounced in the black community. All of this is purposefully done to create conflict so that we fight against each other over ideology or political party. Meanwhile the deceivers profit from our confusion. We are too busy looking for enemies so that we overlook our allies.

Black conservatives are not the enemy of other black people, we are merely people who see a different path for success, but we ultimately want the same results. Many black Americans complain about substandard living in urban areas but vote for the same politicians, the same political party and the same policies that have led to this urban poverty. While many of us don't trust the government, we somehow see our only path to success being through the government. But this only produces more bloated programs that enrich the political establishment.

Political and social manipulation has fed into our own victimization with increasing black-on-black suspicion of political and social betrayal. This suspicion has demonized social conservatism and the role of God in black America when it used to be the norm. This ploy may have worked, but it is reversible as long as we realize who the puppet masters really are who are pulling our strings.

- CHAPTER 11 -

OVER RELIANCE ON GOVERNMENT

The government has a variety of functions that are necessary in American society. The most essential functions involve ensuring national defense and protecting our borders from foreign invaders. The government also establishes regulations that curb abuse from private industry and sets laws that help to protect an individual's liberty. Ideally, these duties should be the primary focus of the government, but increasingly the government has become more of a hindrance in American life than a benefit.

Most of the major issues that affect us nationwide have resulted from the government believing that they are trying to help us when in fact they are hurting us. The larger the federal government grows, the more wasteful and inefficient it becomes. Our state governments aren't much better with the amount of overreach they practice on a daily basis in attempting to dictate their citizens' lives.

For the most disadvantaged among us, life revolves primarily around the alleged generosity of the state which has become their provider, protector and enabler. We have whole families who have grown up with the entitlement of government supervision to survive. We all know of these people who have become so dependent on the state controlling their life that they believe that they are incapable of such control.

In the most extreme situations, they live in government housing, are fed through state food programs, and rely on public transportation. For those who grow up in such an environment, self-reliance has disappeared and all we see are people who are being victimized by the government. They wake up surrounded by the bare minimum in living standards and hope to not hear any scratching in the walls from the rodents that reside alongside them or see anything scurrying away when they turn on the lights.

When they leave their building, they realize that danger lurks around the corner and a sense of fear creeps in when they see a group of rambunctious black youth gathered nearby.

They feel the relief of escaping from possible danger, but that turns into disappointment as they wait for their local bus to show up. They face a public transportation system that is consistently late and inadequate in the service it provides for their community. The bus finally arrives, and they see the look of disregard on the driver's face because his check is guaranteed by the state and the union protects the unpunctual. The faded seats on the bus are filled by those who have faded in their belief that they can do better than their current situation, so they hopelessly ride along the government mandated routes until they reach their destination.

Their government provided cell phone vibrates in their pocket, alerting them of what always seems to be negativity, ranging from the inevitable low bank balance alert or a loved one expressing their daily dysfunction. As the bus rides along, they peer through the window and view their community's chaos that has been subsidized by the government.

Though they are late, they finally arrive at their destination - their local failing government-run public school. They see their child standing in front of a dilapidated building masquerading as a school with a look of disappointment. This unfortunately is their normal facial expression after attending such a failure. When inquiring about their day, they are given a description of a place where no one cares about the future of the children that roam its premises - neither the children nor the adults.

They describe a classroom experience where teachers are either late, don't show up, or don't care. They describe situations in which a teacher who wants to do the right thing can't because they are hindered by administrative bureaucracy, old textbooks, or no supplies to teach effectively. They describe a building that is physically falling apart and barely functional.

But they can't help but notice that their school's principal is driving in luxury. They know that the more their children fail, the more money their broken schools receive. However, it wasn't until that moment that they realized where that money was actually going.

Hunger creeps upon them, prompting them to seek out food that is affordable instead of nutritional. After selecting a meal providing short-lived nourishment, they hand the cashier a card with the letters "EBT". With every swipe of their card, they lose even more of their independence. The cashier hands the card back while wondering if they are facing someone who is truly in need or a leech on the system. The latter is what will be assumed.

With poor nutrition follows poor health, leading them to their local urgent care to examine the internal damage that has been done. They hand the receptionist proof that the government is helping to keep them alive by providing their Medicaid insurance card. Moments later, the results of their substandard living are reported by their physician and it's not good news. A feeling of shame permeates as they feel trapped in an economic situation that limits them to fewer healthy foods because they reside in a neighborhood that lacks nearby options for healthy living - better known as a food desert.

With disappointing news comes a disappointed posture as they walk hand in hand with their child. A day that they wish could be forgettable is remarkably like the day before and the day before that. With phone in hand, they begin to call a friend for comfort but that comfort disappears along with their phone into the hands of a thief.

Too tired to run, they shout for help, which never comes in a timely fashion. The authorities are nearby but choose not to yield to their emergency. These officers have been put in a position to choose whether to interact with the public with the risk of harsh scrutiny or to sit idly by to minimize their personal risk. They chose the latter. The assumption of protection from the government has marked another government failing that greatly impacts their life.

After a day of defeat, they return to the housing that the government supplies for them. Their child falls asleep but is unable to fully rest due to the stress of their daily existence. As they lay their head upon the pillow, the sound of gunfire coming from outside rather than the noise of crickets chirping. They wonder if one day they will be the victim of such crime. What would they be able to do to defend themself? They have already witnessed the lack of protection from government funded police. And they realize that they are also powerless within their own home. The government housing authority has restricted them from legally owning a gun while living in such a jungle. They are the innocent among terrorists, and the government's rules help to embolden daily terrorism against the poor.

They frequently see the results of a new black-market economy of depravity surrounding drugs. They know that the strung-out vessels that lurk around them have found a way to game the government system, and their drug habit has become subsidized by the governmental paternalism. The gunfire that they hear at night is fueled by such an industry, creating a war for territory and economic control among the various factions of terrorists.

Many of us know people who live in these circumstances, often because they have no other options. The reality for the person that I described is that the government has placed them in a position of dependence, not empowerment. Imagine being this person and waking up to the fact that you are essentially a slave to the government's goodwill. You look around to see that you own nothing, you do nothing for yourself, and the government is perfectly willing to help you stay economically sedated. The world around you is frantically moving, yet you are perpetually sitting still, waiting for someone to do for you what you believe you are incapable of.

We call the American welfare system "temporary" yet we have generations of families that find a way to stay on it in one way or another for decades. For those who want to leave the system, they struggle over this decision because it feels as if there is no gradual return to the workforce. If you cross the financial threshold even by a dollar, your governmental parents cut you off and many are unwilling to sacrifice even substandard living to achieve this independence.

Giving people continual government money keeps them from being a productive member of the American workforce. The more those in power try to help, the more the poor suffer. The government pumps billions of dollars into failing school districts based on their poor test scores, but they are only incentivizing their failure, not their success. Where is the oversight for these public slush-funds in urban areas? It is all about politics, and politics always comes first over the potential success of the children.

Baltimore for example, ranked as one of the poorest cities in the U.S.. Only 13 percent of the Baltimore City Public Schools' fourth graders tested at or above proficient in reading in 2019 and 2017. Yet they receive the most funding per pupil in the state of Maryland - $16,184 per pupil in 2017. This is the third highest level of per pupil spending in the country (based on U.S. Census). Where is this money actually going? Why is the government incentivizing failure?

The government believes it is helping families by paying single mothers more money per child. But they are incentivizing reckless sexual behavior and careless family planning. The epidemic of fatherless children within the black community is being subsidized by the same government institutions that claim to care about black families.

The government writes laws restricting black Americans in urban areas from possessing guns legally. They create bureaucratic hurdles for law-abiding citizens that make the cost of legal ownership unappealing and unaffordable. How can we have a successful family outcome in such dangerous places if we are unable to protect ourselves adequately? These questions never get answered because the government doesn't bother to respond to such commonsense inquiries.

Despite the failures of constant government intervention, many black Americans are perfectly fine with an ever growing and intrusive local and federal government. The government hand that feeds you will always find a way to take away from you. The political establishment has made black Americans take their eyes off of the real culprit causing their problems.

This has been occurring for multiple generations as we are encouraged to focus on the identity of others and compare themselves to them, so they don't notice the greed of the few at the top.

Men like Martin Luther King Jr. weren't just fighting against the racism that existed in America. They were also fighting against the government and its powerful apparatus of control. The government then as now was separating Americans from each other on the basis of identity. The government oppressed black Americans with approval from the collective. And the government continues to create and benefit from racial division.

We may believe now that the fight is over with the government. But the reality is that the strategy of warfare has changed, not ended. The strategy of the government, mainly from leftist Democrats, was to move away from overt oppression of blacks to more elusive tactics of subversion. The political establishment understood that they had to keep their enemies closer than their friends. Thus, they have been working to create a population of submissive blacks who will vote for their arch-nemeses, the Democrat elite.

We were told the lie that economic and social progress could only happen for blacks if we had more black representation in government. We are supposed to look at black government officials as one of us so that we don't realize that what has happened is the promotion of a black person into the elite ruling class. Their race is only a tool for greater manipulation of black people. That black politician who you fawned over is now part of the upper ruling class and they collude with the economic elite daily.

Black members of the political establishment know how to weaponize their blackness because they grew up in a community that did it routinely.

They don't care about your legitimate concerns. You serve them now, not vice versa. Thieves don't always sneak through your window at night, they also wear suits and live in Washington D.C.. Political thievery comes in all shades and genders in government, yet we are blindly stuck on their racial identity rather than their class.

Racism is the poor man's distraction from examining class. True intersectionality has nothing to do with race or gender, it is the intersectionality between government and private industry as they seek more favorable corporate welfare in the form of bailouts, subsidies or reforms that benefit them in exchange for campaign contributions, board positions for the children of politicians and various other methods of corruption.

Barack Obama once made a modest living as a community organizer and is now jet-setting with billionaires like Richard Branson. The majority of his career was in government and now he's estimated to have a net worth of over 40 million dollars. Are we to believe that this was all achieved without a speck of corruption? Ask yourself why a Wall Street firm would pay Obama $400,000 to give a speech immediately after he left his presidency? One can only speculate.

As Americans were losing their jobs and homes due to the reckless behavior of Wall Street, your black President left everyone out to dry with no punishment for the elite who gambled the average person's life savings away. Picture all the poor people who threw their modest life savings into a deposit for a home that they couldn't afford. Now they were left with no financial safety net and no home.

Where was your black President when thousands of black families were forced out of their homes? He was in private meetings negotiating deals to give the criminals on Wall Street more capital by means of bailouts and accepting pinky promises that they wouldn't do it again. Where was the justice for the average American who now had to suffer because of the actions of a few in the top economic class?

Black Americans cried more when Barack Obama was elected than when the economy crashed in 2008. Our desire to see someone who looked like us overshadowed the subtle signs of his being corruptible, inexperienced, and someone who didn't keep his promises. In other words, a typical politician. We were and are stuck in the mindset of identity politics thinking that Barack Obama is a black politician rather than a politician who happens to be black.

Even more to the point, he was an ambitious man who relished his elite status over sympathy with the common black folk. Barack Obama is no different than the next politician who plays by the rules of giving favors to his donors. Do you honestly think that a man who graduated from Columbia and Harvard Universities doesn't believe he's elite or find some sort of kinship with the elite?

The intersection between government and private industry during the 2008 financial crisis allowed the government to create the environment in which Wall Street manufactured bad loans that would ultimately fail. In an article published by CBS News titled "Here's what really caused the housing crisis", they detail effectively what caused the chaos from the very beginning.

"Under Clinton's Housing and Urban Development (HUD) secretary, Andrew Cuomo, Community Reinvestment Act regulators gave banks higher ratings for home loans made in 'credit-deprived' areas. Banks were effectively rewarded for throwing out

sound underwriting standards and writing loans to those who were at high risk of defaulting.

What's more, in the Clinton push to issue home loans to lower income borrowers, Fannie Mae and Freddie Mac made a common practice to virtually end credit documentation, low credit scores were disregarded, and income and job history was also thrown aside. The phrase "subprime" became commonplace. What an understatement. … Tragically, when prices fell, lower-income folks who really could not afford these mortgages under normal credit standards, suffered massive foreclosures and personal bankruptcies."

This plan by the government was intended to be a form of reparations for minorities and low-income Americans who had dreamed of owning a home. Yet it only hurt them in the long run. Every time the government tries to help black people specifically on the basis of race, it ends up hurting us. Instead of helping to create an environment where we can create our own wealth, they lower the standards because they believe we are incapable of meeting them. Instead of removing the governmental restrictions that prevent us from prospering, they give us handouts and write laws that prevent us from achieving due to our own hard work. One of these restrictions that we are told will help black folk are minimum wage laws. Interestingly when these laws were first written they were used specifically to drive out the lower skill black work force.

"Minimum-wage laws can even affect the level of racial discrimination. In an earlier era, when racial discrimination was both legally and socially accepted, minimum-wage laws were often used openly to price minorities out of the job market." – Thomas Sowell / NY Post Article "Why racists love minimum wage laws."

"The history of black workers in the United States illustrates the point. From the late nineteenth-century on through the middle of the twentieth century, the labor force

participation rate of American blacks was slightly higher than that of American whites. In other words, blacks were just as employable as the wages they received as whites were at their very different wages. The minimum wage law changed that. Before federal minimum wage laws were instituted in the 1930s, the black unemployment rate was slightly lower than the white unemployment rate in 1930. But then followed the Davis-Bacon Act of 1931, the National Industrial Recovery Act (NIRA) of 1933 and the Fair Labor Standards Act (FLSA) of 1938 – all of which imposed government-mandated minimum wages, either on a particular sector or more broadly.

The National Labor Relations Act of 1935, which promoted unionization, also tended to price black workers out of jobs, in addition to union rules that kept blacks from jobs by barring them from union membership. The NIRA raised wages in the Southern textile industry by 70 percent in just five months and its impact nationwide was estimated to have cost blacks half a million jobs. While this Act was later declared unconstitutional by the Supreme Court, the FLSA was upheld by the High Court and became the major force establishing a national minimum wage." – Economist Thomas Sowell's book "Basic Economics: A common sense guide to the economy"

"After minimum wage rates were raised sharply, the unemployment rate shot up for both white and black teenagers. Even more significantly, an unemployment gap opened between the rates for white and black teenagers…. We regard the minimum wage rate as one of the most, if not the most, antiblack laws on the statute books. The government first provides schools in which many young people, disproportionately black, are educated so poorly that they do not have the skills that would enable them to get good wages. It then penalizes them a second time by preventing them from offering to work for low wages as a means of inducing employers to give them on-the-job training. All in the name of helping the poor." – Economist Milton Friedman's book "Free to Choose"

These economists are illustrating the point that the government's strength along with their supposed compassion in increasing the minimum wage has directly impacted employment opportunities for the least skilled and has altered the normal behavior of employers. The government imposing a minimum market value for human labor only leaves the least skilled out on the streets and reduces the amount of job opportunities overall for a working labor force.

Thomas Sowell even points out how these types of laws were used tactically all over the world by racists in unions to lock out blacks from certain labor markets. No amount of collusion by private industry could enforce such a racialized lockout without the participation of the government. Coincidentally, the best jobs that are available today in many lower-income black urban city centers are unionized and likely within the government.

Politicians are throwing around the idea of monetary reparations as a ploy to keep black Americans engaged in the political process, but what impact would it have? Remember, the government doesn't make money; it takes money. Is it fair for the government to take other people's money to pay back present day black Americans who were never enslaved? How much money is slavery worth in dollars anyway?

How would this work exactly? Only half of my bloodline is descended from slaves. Do I get half of the reparations? Would we need DNA tests to prove our ancestry? What about people who are multi-racial?

If we were to look at the long history of the government giving black people handouts, we can anticipate that reparations would be a disastrous mess. For one, we all know that a reparations bill would be a cash grab for special interest groups. This money wouldn't be coming from our own treasury since our country is constantly in debt. It would most likely be more borrowed from the federal reserve. The printing of more currency would increase the likelihood of the inflation of the U.S. dollar. There are about 1.2 million black Americans in the United States. Thus, any reparations of a significant amount, let's say in the thousands of dollars per person, would require billions of dollars of federal spending in the form of one-time payments.

There is only so much you can do with a singular payment and in the long run, that money will be gone, and we would still be in the same place, or possibly in a worse situation. Plus, the likelihood of inflation would result in less buying power for all of us. What will happen once that money disappears? Do we believe people will be satisfied with one reparation payment?

Politicians will likely use historical black suffering from slavery as an excuse to continually write laws that give a fraction to black people and the majority to their corrupt cronies. If the year 2020 has shown us anything, it is that when large stimulus bills are passed in the name of helping the average American, said Americans get the crust and special interest gets the rest of the pie.

The topic of reparations isn't about if it could actually happen, it's about should it happen. Should the government sanction money for those who weren't directly affected by slavery? The time to handout money to black people passed generations ago. Giving someone like me money that was unearned doesn't help me in the long run. It is a momentary lottery win that will inevitably fade away.

How would non-blacks feel about an overt sanctioning of money specifically based on race? This question matters because we would undoubtedly be siphoning money away from non-black Americans to finance this venture. In 1865, the year that slavery was abolished, the United States had a population of about 35 million people, today we have a population of about 331 million (U.S. Census). Also keep in mind that there were 15 slave states versus the 19 free states, and slave owners were an obvious minority within the slave states.

The point of mentioning these figures is to highlight the expansion of the population within the United States, especially due to immigration, meaning that the vast amount of present-day U.S. Citizens has zero lineage with anyone who owned slaves or participated in the slave trade in the United States. Is it fair to penalize those who have no slave-holding lineage or American lineage that predates the abolishment of slavery?

A possible rebuttal to this question might be that all Americans should pay reparations because they benefited from systemic racism. But why should the average person pay for the sins of the ruling elite who made up the government at the time? It was the system of government institutions that made slavery possible. The government was the only system that could legalize slavery and Jim Crow. The ruling elite always use the might of the government to change the rules of the game at the citizens' expense. Who do you think owned those slaves? Poor white rednecks? Laws aren't passed unless they benefit someone. So, ask yourself, who benefited from slavery? Who benefited from segregation? Who benefits from racial strife today? The powerful elite does.

When the political establishment, mainly Democrats, want to restrict your right to protect yourself, they use black crime as a justification to create more restrictive gun laws. When the political establishment wants to prop-up the private prison industry for their lobbyist friends, they will create unbalanced laws at the expense of black Americans. When the government wanted to extend COVID-19 lockdowns, they legitimized their totalitarian actions by invoking COVID health statistics of black people. When you see failing black city after failing black city, you will probably find government corruption peaking around the corner.

Government corruption has no distinct color, and we have allowed men and women to ruin our communities indiscriminately because they are part of the blackness cult leadership. They slide into failing neighborhoods; claim they are just like you as they pull up in their Mercedes and walk out the back door with their pockets filled with your tax dollars.

Many of these cities have a revolving door of black leadership that always promises to help make a change for "their people". Meanwhile, decade after decade, nothing changes. That's because "their people" are actually their friends within government, powerful business associates and contractors, and anyone else who fits within their tax bracket.

Former Mayor of New Orleans, Ray Nagin, was convicted of corruption. Former Mayor of Baltimore, Sheila Dixon, was convicted of embezzlement. Former Mayor of Atlanta, Bill Campbell, was convicted of tax evasion. Former Mayor of Birmingham, Larry Langford, was convicted of accepting bribes in exchange for giving $7.1 million in sewer-bonds to one of his friends. Former Mayor of Dallas, Don Hill, was sentenced to 18 years in prison for leading a massive shakedown scheme. All were black politicians from largely black cities.

This list can go on and these are only the government officials who were actually caught. The list is bountiful with examples of shady deals that are questionable in their legality. This list only consists of black Mayors (mostly from cities with black majorities) but who knows how many other black state representatives, councilmen, or federal representatives have been using their influence to enrich themselves.

The government as a whole and our state and federal representatives, including black representatives, are not the saviors of black Americans. The government has been know to strangle black progress for the purposes of tax extortion and to gain votes. When extortion doesn't work, they use social bribery by means of welfare or other failing social programs and they keep you in line by leveraging your blackness for their own agenda.

With more social programs comes more tax money taken from the people. With more money at their disposal, the more power the politicians hold. The more power they hold, the easier they are to corrupt. The more corruptible they are, the more wealth inequality will increase.

If the government has less power, then less harm can be done to its citizens. When we see corporations getting bailouts, policies changing in favor of those in power, and lobbyists literally drafting new legislation in back rooms, this is not capitalism, this is crony-capitalism.

When you believe that the sins of our past, including slavery, were due to capitalism, you are not understanding what capitalism is. Capitalism, in basic terms, is a voluntary exchange of goods and services that benefit both parties. There is nothing voluntary about unpaid labor by means of force. Our founding fathers stated that all men are created equal. But the government was used to enforce inequality after our country's creation despite the intentions of many of the founders.

Our over-reliance on the government is not sustainable for our individual long-term success. We need to seriously reconsider how involved we want to continue to be with our true historical abuser - the government and those in authority.

- CHAPTER 12 -

THE NORMALIZATION OF BLACK DEATH

"Someone is shot in Chicago every three hours and 16 minutes. There is a human that dies from gunshots in Chicago every 18 hours. That is all week, every week, so far in 2015."

– Metrospirit

"Today's Chicago More Dangerous For Blacks Than The Lynching South"

Black death is tragically abundant. Yet we are passive in the face of these statistics. This is not always intentional or malicious. We may not intend to ignore the rising numbers of dead black people that fill our morgues far too early in life. However, our passivity gives it normalcy.

Out of all racial demographics, black Americans have the shortest life expectancy (according to the CDC) and we die primarily in ways that are preventable. Homicide is the leading cause of death for black men between the ages of 1 to 19 (35%) and 20 to 44 (27%) and is the fourth leading cause for black males of all ages. For comparison's sake, for white men, homicide ranks fourth between the ages 1 to 19 (4.9%) and fifth between ages 20-44 (2.9%). White men are more likely to kill themselves than be killed by someone else.

We know who is killing us with such frequency. I don't need to give you any statistics about that because it's fairly obvious. If we are honest, we know that our greatest danger today isn't the white man, nor is it a racist white cop, it is ourselves. For all races, violence is overwhelmingly committed by someone from the victim's own racial group. But the rate at which blacks commit violence against each other is the ultimate concern.

The phrase "black on black crime" has been politicized and demonized as being racist jargon. But this does not remove its truthfulness regardless of how it may offend your sensibilities. It has become apparent that we would rather pretend that this extreme rate of death is normal rather than acknowledging the problem and attempting to change it.

We do not inherit violent tendencies. We learn them. Once they are learned, it is a matter of whether the surrounding culture comes to accept violence as a means of resolution. To accept violence, you don't need to signal that you're okay with it, you just simply do nothing about it. The lack of desire to vilify perpetrators simply because their skin color matches our own is an abhorrent justification for our neglect. This way of thinking lowers our community's expectation of abiding by the same rules as everyone else. This has resulted in frequent murderous conflicts throughout this country.

If we expect violence to occur in black urban areas, why would anyone else expect differently? We cannot place expectations upon the majority when we lack expectations for ourselves. The existence of the crime infested black ghetto is part of the cycle of degradation that has continued decade after decade. Instead of putting our foot down and taking our community back from the ways of immorality, we normalize black villainy and categorize it as part of the black experience.

Why do we glorify our villains and ignore the innocent who are caught in between? Why is glorification more palatable than judging the culture that excuses felonious behavior? We excuse our villains when we pay more attention to their court appearances than their school appearances. We excuse our villains when we would rather pay their bail than a college fund. We excuse our villains when we claim that their imprisonment is rooted in racism or the continuation of slavery from over a century ago.

How do we glorify our villains? We believe that dressing like them makes us more culturally relevant and that taking part in a lifestyle which involves high risk and immoral behavior is something that isn't shameful. Without the social pressure to conform to a more moral lifestyle, our black youth are being turned into urban terrorists who risk death while causing death.

We have become selective with our outrage depending on which black person dies and under which circumstance they perish. The only people who seem to care are the ones who are emotionally close to the victims of violence. Outside of these few, they are just another dead black body, waiting to be buried, alongside our expectations of prosperity for our black youth.

Black death has become normalized to the point of becoming entertainment in America. Television shows like "The First 48" encapsulate the routine nature of the murder of black men. Perhaps this show can be viewed as educating us on how bad things are in certain cities or on the process of solving a crime. However, the fact that a television production team can sit still in a police station and know that another black body will roll through in a matter of days should alarm us. Yet we do not lose any sleep over it.

This type of television programming should cause sadness and alarm at the loss of life and loss of freedom. Instead, it simply causes us to grab another bag of popcorn. If you take more than one minute to think about what you are watching, you will understand that the camera is displaying the collapse of black morality in a select city near you.

Many of us don't think about it because we don't want to experience the guilt of sleeping in a warm bed and not worrying about a stray bullet penetrating our walls. We live comfortably, not worrying that a trivial conflict will turn into a shooting that results in a body bag and our name in print on the local television station. We know not to cross over to the other side of the tracks because that's none of our business. But we listen to the music made by the people from the other side and curiously watch from a distance as their bodies are carted away for our entertainment.

All of this trauma just feels so normal to us that we just don't question it. Is this the way it is supposed to be for us? Why is it only us who live in this chaos? These are complex questions that require complex answers. But who has the stomach for that? Many of us don't care to question and just accept this as normal. America has gravitated to the assumption that this is what is supposed to happen, so why change it? Why attempt to save our children when their life is meant to be at risk? Why encourage peaceful resolution when chaos is our state of being? Why attempt to save a life when we have been encouraged to sacrifice an unborn life? There are few answers given to these disturbing questions about how we conduct ourselves and what we expect from ourselves.

Friday May 1st, 2020 – Calvin Munerlyn, a security guard for a Detroit Dollar General, was at the entrance of the store making sure that everyone entering the premises was following the state mandate to wear face masks during the COVID-19 virus pandemic. During his shift he encountered a woman, Sharmel Teague, and her child attempting to enter the store. Calvin prevented them from entering because her daughter did not have a face mask.

He was a 43-year-old family man just trying to do his job but after this interaction, his life came to a tragic end. After their verbal altercation, Teague left and returned with 2 men, her husband and son, Larry Edward Teague and Ramonyea Bishop. Larry came into the store to yell at Calvin for disrespecting his wife, and then Bishop senselessly shot Calvin in the head, killing him. After this tragic event, Calvin's cousin, Tina James said something that we hear all too frequently after black homicides yet no one seems to adhere to: "This is not the way to do things right now. We need to come together."

When this news came out, it received national attention for a day or so, and only because it was related to COVID-19. If this conflict were not about mask enforcement gone wrong, no one would know about it or care. Some of you reading this may not have even heard of this story or recognize his name. There is a good reason for it. It is because black murder committed by black hands is not newsworthy and doesn't trigger a reaction for outrage, no matter how horrific the circumstance.

Calvin was a father and a husband. He left behind a family and not as a result of his own doing. How come strangers care more about his death than so-called black leaders and organizations? It is very clear. Black on black violence is not profitable or exploitable. We must ask ourselves the question, do black lives really matter? Activists virtually never show up for black people dying unless it fits a narrative that is exploitable. Black death is far more profitable when the finger on the trigger is pale and not dark.

Black organizers and so-called black leaders invoke the "do not believe your lying eyes" doctrine when the perpetrators are one of our own. Acknowledging that there is a problem would expose the fact that throughout the decades of so-called black leadership, black people have regressed morally in some of the most economically hurt cities in America.

There is a major crisis with our young black men who lack the ability to regulate their emotions and their manufactured pride. Calvin's murder was one of those preventable deaths that I mentioned earlier. If his assailant had practiced a moderate amount of conflict resolution, Calvin would be walking around today. A lack of care for human life permeates many within the black community.

Why do we shrug our shoulders when men like Calvin die? Why have we given up on promoting the love of God for our young men? Why do we accept cowardly policies like "no snitching" when one of our own is killed?

We have been trained to say "it is what it is" because that absolves us of any responsibility to change the situation. We are told that the root causes of these crimes are racism, slavery, colonization, redlining, or a mixture of all of them. In what way does structural racism force a man like Bishop to grab a gun and shoot an innocent man without conscience?

We have given up trying to change this continual violence because it takes away from the narrative that we are constantly told, which is that white racism is our greatest danger today. If this were true, why is it that black millionaires don't live in the hood with other black people? Why is it that they buy homes in majority white neighborhoods? They have the means to go where they choose, yet they don't choose to stay in places with people that look like me.

Why would the top black earners put their own children in danger of white racists when it would be easier to send them to a black majority school in urban areas? It is because the real genuine danger lies within our black communities. Wealthy blacks would much rather risk the possibility of someone being insensitive because of their color than of potentially taking a bullet if they were to choose to live near people of their color.

We have turned our backs on promoting God to our young black men, and it has resulted in them gravitating towards devilish deeds with prideful insecurities. A secure man doesn't choose violence in moments when de-escalation is possible. A godly man chooses to protect others instead of inflicting pain upon others. While we have been focused on being unapologetically black, we have taken our eye off what is truly important, being unapologetically moral.

The removal of moral standards has contributed to the removal of black lives. To maintain a moral culture, we must be willing to be principled enough to criticize bad ideas and perhaps even shame those within our communities who deviate from healthy cultural norms. We need to have the courage to do this even to those within our own group, or in this case, race.

If you stand for nothing, you'll fall for anything. If you don't stand against the carnage that is happening against our black brothers and sisters, then you'll fall into the trap of normalizing our demise. You must be willing to speak out when everyone is choosing to be silent. You must be willing to risk losing relationships with people you love to live with yourself morally.

You must be willing to question tenets of the group culture if they sway you away from godly tenets.

The activists among us believe they are fighting for righteousness when they protest the death of a singular man or woman, but the vast majority of them are practicing selective morality. The same people who are outraged by the death of Michael Brown care nothing about the death of Calvin Munerlyn.

When 77-year-old retired police captain David Dorn was killed during the George Floyd riots as he was protecting a friend's business, black people were silent. As his dead body was broadcast live on the internet people were quiet because it did not fit into their political narrative because he was murdered by another black man over a television. Activists would rather reimagine the lives of career criminals that died in part due to their own actions than highlight the truly innocent who died with honor and without malice.

It is not only the death of black males that is alarming, but also the black boys and girls who are never given a voice against their own execution. They are the black boys and girls who were never given a chance to argue for their existence because our laws have legalized and normalized their deaths. I am referring to the genocide of black children that has been happening for decades through legalized abortion.

Genocide is defined as the systemic killing of a racial or cultural group. Every racial group in America participates in abortion to some degree. However, for black women, the abortion rate compared to our population size is alarming. I have great concern over our acceptance of this immoral activity simply due to its legality.

In 2017, there was an estimate of 870,000 black pregnancies, but 33.9% of them resulted in abortions (CDC). Just to compare, there were 2,331,000 white pregnancies and 12% of them resulted in abortions. Black women are about 13% of the female population and they had 34.7% of the abortions in 2017. White women make up 60% of the female population and had 32.9% of the abortions in 2017. From 1965 to 2018, the estimated abortions by black women in comparison to current population is 42%, resulting in the murder of 18.7 million black babies and counting.

Something is clearly wrong when over a third of our black babies are being killed by their mothers. Something is wrong within our culture when we see abortion as another form of birth control. There is clearly a disconnect from our moral principles when we sacrifice the life of our children to satisfy our selfish desires. Women are given the amazing ability to procreate. Yet our black women have renounced their first responsibility as a mother, which is to protect their children.

The women are not solely to blame because the men who impregnate them sometimes don't fight hard enough to convince the women not to contribute to the genocide. I can say this because at one point in my life, I was this man. I was the man that stood with a blank stare as his sexual partner told him the news that he was about to be a father. When the following question came about from her mouth "What are we going to do?" I cowardly stated, "I support whatever you want to do." At that moment, I failed as a father who is supposed to protect his child by convincing the mother that everything will be alright.

I had allowed fear to creep in instead of being a man and fighting for my child. I had put the mother's rights above my child's rights. I was supposed to speak up for my child, but I remained silent as the decision to execute him or her was made. I cowardly sat in the car as my child was disposed of as if it were trash. Much of my cowardly attitude stemmed from the leftist messaging that I was surrounded with that convinced me to be pro-choice instead of pro-morality.

As I sat in the car waiting for her to return, I asked myself, "If giving her the choice to have an abortion is the right thing, why do I feel so wrong about this?" I try my best to not live with regret as I tend to find life lessons even in my failures, but this situation still haunts me years later. Though I am not the one who had the abortion, I stood by and did nothing to attempt to stop it, making me just as culpable for the murder.

Once she returned to the car, we drove to her home in silence, and I didn't dare to discuss what had just happened. As we drove, she couldn't help but break down into tears as she was already regretting her decision. We held each other at that moment, realizing how we had failed to do the right thing for our child.

When we discuss the topic of abortion, the focus is always on the women's wants and the men have ultimately no say. We have become so flippant about the unborn being murdered because we can't stare them in the eyes as we end their life. We also never discuss the emotional impact this decision makes. Women who choose to abort feel a sense of loss and continue to question themselves as a mother, even if they birth children later in their lives. No amount of time can fully repair that feeling of being broken enough to sanction the execution of an innocent offspring.

We never consider the men who witness this event and have no recourse to try to stop it from occurring. Though I am regretful that I didn't fight for my child, I also know that even if I did, I would have had no legal recourse to stop the mother from committing such an atrocity. If my child were born, I would have half the legal say in what happens to them, but as long as they are within the womb, the father's voice ultimately means nothing. The women's movement that has prioritized women above men has created this situation, making her desires more relevant than the father's, yet I was equally responsible for the child's existence.

Sadness still affects me, and I often pray in hopes that God can forgive me for my participation in such sinfulness. At that time in my life, I was lost religiously, holding onto my agnostic identity and forgetting my Christian morality when it was convenient to the situation. My lack of a relationship with God opened the door for me to forgo my Christian morality for politically correct expediency and to allow me to bow to matriarchal demands instead of God's will.

I now realize the amount of indoctrination that happens within the black community that enables black women to seek empowerment through all family decision making, including deciding who lives and who dies. Our strong black women are being taught to carry out four major roles now that the black father is mostly absent from the home: financier, caregiver, juror and executioner.

I can be critical of these actions, but I am not completely judgmental towards the women that go through this process because I understand that there is an abortion propaganda war, and black women are one of the targets. Men are supposed to be a good person by considering the feelings of women regardless of the fact that it is hurting someone else, like a baby. You are supposed to redefine what a child is to alter the reality of such inhumane practices. You're supposed to negate your responsibility as a parent to fulfill other people's political motives.

Leftists have manipulated black women into sacrificing their morals and have strategically shamed black men with claims of misogyny if they appear to challenge the women's decision. If you are a woman and you are pro-life, then you are painted as someone who takes away from women rather than as someone advocating to save a child's life, or dare I say, even your own child's life.

By nearly every measurable statistic, it is clear that there is something wrong when an extreme minority is outpacing the majority in preventable deaths. We are volunteering disproportionately to end our children's lives through abortion. And if they are one of the 2/3rds of black pregnancies that result in childbirth, we are raising them in environments that no longer believe in true discipline or teach appropriate conflict resolution. Even in their tragic deaths, the no snitching policies emphasize how much we don't really care.

In Chicago (2019), the percentage of African American murders that are solved was the lowest among any other racial group at 22%. Do we care that the families of the 78% may never get justice or know who took their loved ones away from them?

We would rather protect ourselves and play cover for the terrorists roaming our streets than sacrifice our comfort to seek justice. It doesn't help that in many of these dangerous cities there are such harsh restrictions on legal gun ownership that people can't even attempt to protect themselves. This leaves the criminals as the only ones who are armed and the police afraid to aggressively patrol for fear of being seen as racist.

The signs are all around us. The numbers don't lie. Yet we still do nothing to change the outcome. Black Americans have chosen to get on their knees and cry over the rare death inflicted by police rather than over the high frequency of tragedy committed against our own people. We only care when the "other" takes one of us. Yet we claim that we are morally justified.

We scream the loudest about justice, but our actions don't back up our claims if one of our own is the perpetrator. We fear monger about the police killing our black youth. But we encourage the execution of a third of them while in the womb for overwhelmingly selfish reasons. Let one white person kill one of us and you will never hear the end of it. But let another black person kill one of us and you will never hear about it.

– CHAPTER 13 –

URBAN TERRORISTS AND CRIMINAL MARTYRS

"One of the tragedies of the struggle against racism is that up to now there has been no national organization which could speak to the growing militancy of young black people in the urban ghetto."

– Stokely Carmichael

In many black communities in America fear makes otherwise logical people comply with the demands of terrorists. People think twice about the colors they wear, what street they decide to walk down, and who they choose to interact with to avoid the potentially deadly wrath of urban terrorists. These terrorists are the few, but they know how to use fear to control the many.

Fear keeps the innocent quiet because they know that retaliation may not only come for them but for those they love. Fear makes the witness blind to what they just witnessed because they have no desire to wear stitches. Leaving this war-torn environment may not be possible due to economics, resulting in compliance for the sake of survival.

Urban terrorists generate profits from the selling of drugs to the sad souls among them to fund their moral corruption. Victims are the byproduct of the chaos. Victimhood is the mental state that the traumatized are unable to escape. From an outsider's perspective, it is a nightmarish dystopia that we wouldn't dare to participate in. But for the innocent who live there, this is life.

The average age of the terrorist declines with every passing generation. Young black boys feel that they have nothing to lose because they already have nothing. Everyone in their life has failed them. The public schools pushed them along without teaching them to satisfy some school administrator's statistics. Uninvolved fathers allowed them to wander aimlessly, trying to find their self-worth. Local politicians section off their neighborhoods from everyone else's and leave them with few opportunities. The media monetizes the community's pain to spread fear and get views, thus scaring away any new economic opportunities.

Terrorists aren't born, they are engineered. They are bred from the failures of a community and neglect from the larger society. The most hardened urban terrorist was once childishly innocent, eagerly waiting to tackle life but unaware that life sometimes hits back. Some of them came from homes so broken that they easily fell through the cracks, never to receive adequate love from their birth parents and falling into the arms of their "adopted" family in the streets.

These are the children of addicts who were sold to the streets in exchange for an endorphin inducing drug. These are young men who either lost or never had a bond with a true masculine figure. They gravitate towards bastardized representations of masculinity including hyper-aggression, extreme pride and limitless egotism.

They are the children who were left to fend for themselves in an environment that is ready to devour the weak. Every possible safety net was pulled away from them and they fell deeper into an unforgiving world of crime, drugs and danger. Instead of their self-esteem being built up, it was crushed by the forces of social neglect.

They meander around life purposeless, depressed and without drive. The choices become fewer and their decision to enter a life of limited outcomes becomes easier. These are young men of desperation who will risk their life just to feel a sense of purpose and belonging.

A male without purpose is neither a man nor a boy, but a motionless soul. Purpose is the adrenaline in the veins of life that keeps us motivated. Without purpose, we are merely vessels waiting for our next task. When boys and men lack direction, the streets become their compass. This newfound compass is magnetized by the desire to take control and flex their dominance over the innocent.

In nature, the vulnerable tend to get devoured by the predator. Likewise, in harsh American ghettos, predators have an appetite for vulnerable young men. The forgotten are encouraged to travel down the path of negative uninhibited behavior until they no longer care about the destructive aftermath that they create. The illusion of power is intoxicating to the formerly weak, allowing them to become the monsters that they used to fear.

A life of family turmoil has been swapped for a new brotherhood that provides the belonging he never had. These gangs portray themselves as a street fraternity for lost boys, promising to fulfill their yearning for unconditional love and purpose as their selling point. Their new family is not respected but feared and seemingly invincible, which attracts any lost child who has been alone and disrespected.

Connection is what they've been seeking since they were born but never received from their real family. To a lost child, the promise of loyalty represents the hope that they will not be discarded again. This new "family" gives them purpose and a reason to wake up in the morning to face the harsh reality that surrounds them.

The process is now complete, and the terror has begun. The collective manipulation to corrupt the innocent has worked. Purpose has been given to the formerly aimless. Whether it is to control territory, a drug market, or people, their assignments always revolve around power.

The need to have control is even stronger for people who have lived years without being able to control what happened to them and who faced unpredictable outcomes. Not knowing where you will sleep, not knowing if you will eat, not knowing if your parents will come home, and not knowing if anyone cares, feed into their desire to control anything that they can get their hands on.

Once they become fully indoctrinated, their social status as loner, loser and neglected is upgraded to feared and terroristic. The lines become blurred between what is right and wrong, whether they act out of survival, greed, pride, or paranoia. They encounter threats from other formerly aimless boys. They fear returning to a state of vulnerability.

The street battles they take part in are motivated by a sense of desperation to never feel powerless again. They are fighting a battle to preserve their power and manhood. And if death is necessary to defend it, so be it. They act like they are invincible but they know that death will come for them sooner rather than later. Their souls died along with their innocence a long time ago, transforming them into fearless provocateurs of death.

The gun is the weapon of choice, the bigger the gun, the bigger his ego. His trigger finger is always itchy and ready to scratch the itch of egotism. He no longer cares about his life, so he has no reason to care about anyone else's. The innocent who gets caught in the crossfire are only casualties of the war that is a constant in their neighborhood. He is unapologetic when his inaccurate aim results in the death of another innocent black child because he also died as a child.

In order to suppress his humanity, he will drink or smoke as much as it takes to no longer feel any kinship to mankind. He must suppress his humanity to excel in his new occupation as a terrorist. Otherwise, he will experience moments of hesitation when committing atrocities. He must consume anything to blind him from the inevitability of his actions, which will result in him either laying in a cell or a casket.

The law is only a mild deterrent because he has no other purpose than to commit terror. Incarceration is just a smaller jungle than the world outside. But in prison the predators are your roommates. The penitentiary becomes frozen in time as the outside world moves forward. His punishment isn't just him losing his freedom. The punishment is also realizing that no one really cares when visitors never come for him.

In too many cases these urban terrorists commute back and forth between two worlds, freedom and isolation. And they repeat the same mistakes over and over that result in transfer from one world to the other. Freedom implies that he has options. But if he doesn't believe those options exist, is he actually free? He has sworn his life to his street family and turning his back on them is not an option. He knows that he's not truly free because death awaits him.

For an urban terrorist, the most honorable way to die is in a manner in which he can be lionized as a martyr, although incidents of martyrdom are rare. He knows that if he is mixed in with the innocent, purely by narrative, that he can be the new American martyr despite his past transgressions. Death by a cop allows him to engineer the legacy that he desires. And his blackness will blind the public when they attempt to peek at his arrest record.

Criminal martyrdom is the ending that every convict would love to have. Martyrdom is the afterlife of honorable men and women who died for a greater good. But the black people that we ordain as martyrs often lived lives that were dishonorable. Their death may have been tragic, and we are all empathetic when anyone is taken too early from this world, but giving unearned praise creates false idols. When you paint their face on the side of buildings or on city streets, you are idolizing them. When there is an elevation of their status to martyrdom, sympathizers will pay the martyr's family respect to show their appreciation for their sacrifice to the political cause.

The boy is brought back to reality as he remembers that martyrdom is rare and what waits for him is much more unpleasant. He believes that his fate has been written in stone, making any alternative destinies nearly impossible. He is angry at the world for allowing him to be abused by his environment when he was too weak to fight back. Terror is his cry for help, but also how he expresses his hatred for humanity. Society must pay for allowing him to become the monster that he feared. He has now become death, the destroyer of the world.

Riddled with trauma, hatred and constant anger, he wants out of his tortured vessel. He grows more reckless because he wants it to all be over. He is conflicted internally as there is a battle between God and himself for ownership of his conscience and the problem is that God is winning. His awakening creates even more self-hatred as he realizes the path of destruction he has left behind him, but he is unable to escape his predetermined path.

The day has come, and he knows what awaits him. The air smells different and the hairs on his arms stand up as if they know what is to come. A sense of vulnerability creeps up on him, making his illusion of fearlessness slip away. He turns his head and sees the barrel of the gun that has been awaiting him for years. The day has come for all his pain to disappear and for his terror to end. The day has come for God to take him away from the hell that he helped to create.

As his body lies on the ground covered in his own blood, he feels the coldness of death. Screaming from sirens and bystanders ensues, but the sound slowly disappears from his eardrums. The light in his eyes fades away into nothingness and his breath becomes thinner. With the last of his breath, he mutters for forgiveness from God and hopes that he is heard.

His body lays motionless as his spirit is carried away - which direction he doesn't know. He has been dreaming for and dreading this moment his whole life, and now the consequences of his actions have caught up to him. All he can hope for is the mercy of God when he casts his final judgment.

His body lays in a casket as both of his families mourn his death. Another dead black man taken too early from this world, caught up in street conflict. Another dead black man that is loved more when he is dead than when he was alive. His body is as cold as his murder case because stitches come for those who snitch, and dead men tell no tales. In the end, his death is just as tragic and unresolved as his life.

America has become passive about the existence of the urban terrorist. We know the chaos that they create, but their existence is not the root of the problem; they are a symptom. We would rather protest for Utopian ideals rather than against the failures of local school districts. We keep voting for politicians that are perfectly fine with there being a divide in resources and treatment within urban areas. We mask these failures as just a piece of the black experience, so we don't attempt to change them. We have no curiosity about how innocence can be corrupted so quickly within our black youth.

In many ways I am empathetic to the urban terrorist because the failures of others during his childhood are what lead them to his lifestyle of depravity. However, my empathy disappears when they become an adult and continue to choose the same actions. We are all to be held responsible for our actions, and the excuse of a terrible childhood doesn't work in the real world. My empathy also diminishes when their lust for power overshadows the safety of others.

The broken family is at the root of the crisis which creates urban terrorists nationwide. Healthy and happy children find no need to engage in dangerous behavior to gain acceptance. Boys with masculine fathers don't need to search for male role models in strangers. They have one at home. The failure of the family structure is the beginning stage that leads to the victimization of the community. The probability of creating an urban terrorist increases with the degree of hurt that children face. As the saying goes, "hurt people hurt people."

– CHAPTER 14 –

BLACK TRAUMA AND RAGE

There have been myriad of traumatic events that have occurred throughout American history against black Americans. There is no denial of this. As children, Americans are taught these historical wrongs in hopes that we will never repeat them and to help us understand that humanity's good nature can quickly deteriorate. The issue isn't that we are taught what happened during the civil rights era or even slavery. The issue is that this is all we are taught.

We are told that we are nothing more than children of struggle who are just lucky that we survived. We are only the descendants of the victimized instead of the overcomers of tyranny. Our history books tell us that our black bodies have only been worthy of servitude and torture. We are reminded that the vast majority of black history was spent waiting for white people to graciously help us, nothing more. Our lessons from history have taught us that black people are America's victim-class who always helplessly extend their hand asking for leniency from their oppressor.

Our group association is with our blackness and blackness requires emotional assimilation. We are encouraged to carry the pain of other black people even if we don't know each other, in effect, if I am punched, we all bruise. The emotional bruising that we carry has been long lasting and slow healing and we all share the trauma of being assaulted. When we read books about the ill treatment of people that resemble us, we assimilate rage against those that presumably hurt our distant relatives.

If we see a black man arrested, it is much like seeing the arrest of one of our cousins. We are taught to transfer emotions between each other, whether it be disappointment, happiness or rage. Transferable black emotions bond us together. This has the potential for positive community association, but it also carries the unhealthy side effect of transferring trauma between us.

With our power to transfer emotions within our group, we also transfer the emotions of those no longer with us, carrying the emotional pain of our predecessors. With the knowledge of black historical pain, we have no choice but to feel their anguish. Our bodies tighten when we envision our ancestors being beaten. We feel as helplessness as a black man surrounded by a mob who is ready to celebrate his lynching. We flinch as we grab our ankles as if we were bitten by a German Shepard in Selma.

We are left to wonder if we are cursed people who were sold by those that looked like us to people who used us. We experience anxiety wondering if after multiple generations of American lineage, this is in fact our home. We wonder why our homeland would treat our ancestors in the manner that it did. But there is no answer that ever feels satisfying. We are ultimately left with the haunting reality that we are stuck with generations of emotional baggage from unhealed people.

I am referring to it as trauma, but we often see it as our legacy. Because we are the descendants of the traumatized, we easily overlook the positive events in black American history and our significant contributions to American society despite what was going on around us. We celebrate the struggle and not how we were able to overcome it. Perhaps this is because pain feels more relatable than relief.

The result of this trained emotional response is to become willingly irrational when we perceive that our distant cousins have been aggrieved. Generations of trauma come out in a variety of ways that can only be described as unapologetically rageful. We may lean harder into superficial thinking by only seeing black and white, making anyone that is not part of our tribe into a suspect. Or we may no longer hold in our emotional anguish and feel the need to express it in ways that we've done countless times before through rioting, looting and burning.

The extreme forms of rage get the most attention because they cause the most physical damage, but I would argue that the lower end of the spectrum is just as damaging to our society. We can rebuild a burned down building, but how do you rebuild trust in white Americans when you have been trained to be skeptical of them?

This skepticism stays with us throughout our daily lives, so that we question the intentions of those we interact with. We become even more racially focused after a publicized interracial incident, not only siding with our tribe but also being fervently curious as to what tribe others are supporting. If you are white and support the white tribe, it must be because of your hatred of the black tribe. However, if a white person chooses the black tribe it must be due to their recognition of black victimhood. If you are white and you throw your support to the black tribe, you will be spared for now. But we will still keep an eye on you because your advocacy might be deception; we still have our skepticism.

Our skepticism of white Americans and America in general prevents us from removing ourselves from the emotional bond we have with our trauma. It prevents us from seeing the good in people and giving the benefit of the doubt to someone who looks different from us. All it takes is for one incident to occur and all our trust disappears, leaving us to only find solace within our tribe. We use skepticism to protect ourselves emotionally and physically, but this skepticism doesn't allow us to heal from our trauma, even if it's transferred trauma.

The extreme forms of black rage have become a form of pornography for our society since we are unable to take our eyes off the chaos that we have created while shamefully wanting more. Once the scent of rage is in the air, the malicious ones appear from the darkness, ready to dance with the devil. The malicious ones go as far as crossing state lines to participate in this intoxicating dance. It comes to a point where you wonder if their rage is based on the reaction to a racialized incident or are they simply devilish opportunists? Either way, their presence is always made known in the form of thievery, destruction and man-made infernos.

During the initial George Floyd riots, we watched a community get torn apart for our lustful entertainment. An already economically hurt area of Minneapolis became barely functional, all out of a desire for vengeance. The extremists that feel such a strong sense of black unification think they are standing up for their black cousin by rioting. But all they are actually doing is stealing from their other black relatives. No one is hurt more by a riot in a black neighborhood than the innocent black people who live there.

The people who believe they are speaking the language of the unheard are taking Martin Luther King's words out of context. They are out of bounds when they believe that the solution to a supposed injustice is another injustice. There are blood, sweat and tears that go into every building and business that they destroy. They are not only stealing merchandise from businesses, but also stealing from families that depend on these businesses for their daily needs. The actions of an extreme few become detrimental to the many and we outsiders watch the mayhem from a distance unaffected.

Those of us who sympathize with or excuse the extremists are as much of a problem as the rioters themselves because they contribute to the lowering of standards that allows black rage to exist. As monolithic as black people tend to be, if there was a monolithic reaction to shame this type of behavior, it wouldn't happen. Safeguards that would prevent this form of extremism are missing because the extremist is the foot soldier for our real-life violent fantasies.

The extremists carry out our guilty pleasure that desires to see someone or something pay for the trauma that we lug around on our shoulders. These are the people who have no moral limiter like most of us have, and we envy their gift of brazenness. We envy how they can show no regard or remorse for their actions. The audacity to look a cop directly in the face and exclaim "fuck the police" must be exhilarating. They are the people that carry out our dirty desires to be publicly naughty, while we are too afraid of exposing ourselves as potential deviants in a civilized society.

But in reality, the extremist is not brave. They are cowards. Cowards hide behind masks as they hurt the innocent. Cowards steal in the name of the dead. Cowards set buildings ablaze in the name of justice. Cowards embrace their victimhood because they fear a life without their security blanket of excuses for their personal failures. Cowards purposely reject treatment to help with their trauma because they are scared that they may find that their shortcomings are theirs alone. The acts of the extremists are not for the black community's benefit but for their own selfish desire to outwardly manifest their victim complex in the most extreme way possible.

The devastation caused by the nationwide George Floyd riots became the most expensive in U.S. History, estimated at between $1-2 billion in insurance claims. For the businesses that survived the riots in Minneapolis, many of them experienced the failure of their local government for not properly protecting what they had worked hard for. Many of these business owners ended up leaving their communities instead of rebuilding. This decision to move resulted in the loss of city tax revenue, local resources and job opportunities for local residents, many of whom were black.

In an article published by The National Review titled *"Why the Economic Scars of Rioting Will Haunt Minneapolis for Decades"*, the author poignantly describes the aftermath caused by overly emotional extremists and opportunists:

"An exodus of businesses is exactly what economists would expect to see in an area ravaged by rioting. The underlying reason is not hard to understand: Property rights are the foundation of any market-based economy. There is a long and clearly observed correlation between the strength of property rights and economic growth.

Why? Well, private enterprise can only function so long as entrepreneurs know they will be reasonably secure in their property. When entire city blocks are destroyed by wanton rioting while local officials sit on their hands, it sends the message that even an otherwise-profitable investment might not pay off. Investors in such cities must now price in economic risk and insecurity that makes it much less competitive compared to its neighbors. And safety considerations also will come into play.

As a result, jobs and economic opportunity are likely to dry up. Property values fall, and the area slips into decline. What's more, higher insurance rates will make doing business more expensive and leave locals facing higher prices. Does that sound like progress to you?"

When we stand by and let extremists misrepresent justice, it is no different from allowing ISIS to decapitate in the name of Islam. Our extremists cut the head off of possible prosperity in already struggling cities, and we don't care to look beyond the chaos of the night. We choose to ignore the people who are left behind, much like the media does when the fires are finally put out and the anger subsides. Our blind eye keeps us from seeing the trauma that is inflicted on already traumatized people.

We are passively fine with black rage even when it's accompanied by white empathetic extremists. We lose our skepticism when white individuals loot black neighborhoods alongside us because extra hands are always welcome when we lead the charge to destroy our own neighborhoods. We don't notice the irony in us claiming that white racism is everywhere as we stand by as white empaths steal from and vandalize black-owned businesses. These riots rarely occur in the suburbs or small-town America, they occur in mostly black sections of urban cities, yet there is no curiosity as to why strange white faces only appear when there is devilish activity taking place.

We have to ask ourselves, has our rage produced outcomes that black Americans can benefit from? Overwhelmingly I would say no. The aftermath of rioting might lead to a deeper investigation, like after the death of Michael Brown in Ferguson, Missouri. But that was likely to occur without the added chaos and the investigation proved that the shooting was justified, which was the opposite of what the rioters wanted.

Riots may also get some politicians to publicly declare that they are with the black community. But they disappear when the cameras do. Rioting is an unproductive method of public disobedience which utilizes acts of terror in hopes of demanding negotiations. But in America, we don't negotiate with terrorists. Terrorism is defined as the unlawful use of violence and intimidation in the pursuit of political aims. This makes rioting for the purpose of political change an act of terrorism.

Among those who do not resort to violence, our internal rage is inflamed and leads to paranoid views of the situation. At a minimum, we become binary thinkers, laser focused on what differentiates us rather than on what can bring us together. We lose sight of the humanity of other people who have different pigmentation as we build a wall in between. This results in an "us vs. them" mentality and ends up making black people into the underdog.

The root of our rage is trauma. Whether it is passed down as generational trauma or personal racial trauma, it needs to be something that we overcome individually and are healed from throughout our community. It is not healthy to carry the emotional baggage of people we don't know, from a time period that we did not live in. This does not mean that we should forget the wrongs. It is imperative that we understand the mistakes of the past to not repeat them.

We have to find a way to forgive, not for the sake of other people but for ourselves. Forgiveness is a virtue that we should seek to attain to remove the burden of victimhood. Forgiveness is what can lead to true social change in American society away from spiteful rage. Martin Luther King Jr. repeatedly talked about the need for forgiveness in American society as he understood its importance in helping to bring social cohesion and to have us live closer to God.

"Forgiveness does not mean ignoring what has been done or putting a false label on an evil act. It means, rather, that the evil act no longer remains as a barrier to the relationship. Forgiveness is a catalyst creating the atmosphere necessary for a fresh start and a new beginning." – Martin Luther King Jr.

– CHAPTER 15 –

THE DISAPPEARANCE OF GOD, SHAME, LOVE AND MORALITY

"For God so loved the world that He gave His only begotten Son, that whoever believes in Him should not perish but have everlasting life."

– John 3:16

What does God actually mean to you? How has God appeared in your life? How has God helped you? Did you reject him when he showed his love? Do you take God for granted?

Throughout most of my life, I struggled to find how God fit into my life, even dating back to my childhood. My relationship with God and religion has been inconsistent, much like many things in my life. I would at times admire those who were able to blindly believe that God was watching them and supporting their every move. Even as a child, I wondered why I was abnormal in a world that appeared to have the answers that I did not possess.

There was one definitive time in my life where I felt God and God's love. It sounds silly, but I was watching a televised sermon and the words from the pastor rang true to me. I remember having the warmth of God's presence in my life and having a sense of being protected. I don't remember my exact age, but I was very young. I'm not sure what happened to that feeling. Maybe it was other events in my childhood, like becoming homeless or constantly moving, that caused that feeling to leave me.

As I entered my teenage years, I saw church as a boring place to go to on Sundays, so I was happy when we didn't attend. Due to us moving around a lot, I never had a consistent church environment and when I would attend, I always felt like a stranger in someone else's home. My skepticism about God's existence grew the older I got. Even with this growing skepticism, I still felt jealous of anyone who could believe in a God that you cannot see or touch.

When I reached my mid-20s, I had a long talk with myself to figure out what I actually believed because my entire life I claimed to be a Christian, but I felt like a fraud claiming a title that I did not deserve. At that point in time, I could not wholly believe that there was no God, much like I couldn't wholly believe in the existence of God. I essentially stayed neutral in the matter, believing in the possibility of God and reserving the right to say, "I don't know." Basically, I identified as Agnostic and felt solace in my new life decision. I no longer felt like a religious fraud and felt comfort in not choosing a particular denomination to call mine.

That should be the end of the story, but it wasn't for me. Like many young people in their 20s, I not only struggled with the question of God, but I struggled with knowing who I am and how to be a man. I became a father at 21 and I had to quickly find the answers to the questions that most people can take their time solving. I now understand that my struggle with myself was the struggle of God trying to make himself known to me.

My 20s was comprised of homelessness, depression, anxiety, panic attacks, agoraphobia, thoughts of suicide, struggling to find a career, the end of my relationship with my father, unemployment, failed relationships and finding the best way to handle all of these matters while being a good father. These were times of ultimate lows, yet I was able to overcome these odds. At my lowest point, I was overweight, unemployed and living in my friend's basement, yet somehow, I was able to overcome all that.

They say that God doesn't give you anything that you can't handle - a phrase that I used to think was bullshit. But I believe it now. I believe in the power of perseverance instead of succumbing to victimhood. My internal struggles with depression and anxiety were me fighting God's will and his ability to give me the strength to overcome. Much like a child, I was stubborn towards my heavenly Father and I chose the hard way and resisted him.

What made me feel his presence more clearly was the constant fortunate coincidences in my life once I stopped letting myself be a victim. For example, I lost my job after 3 weeks of employment, which made me ineligible for unemployment benefits. My old victimized-self would have fallen into depression, but I fought even harder. After 3 months of no income, chasing down job leads and even considering joining the military, I found a position in the career I had been trying to get into for nearly 10 years. It was like God had given me a perseverance test and handed me my reward at the end.

My struggle with God wasn't about finding him, but accepting him. I now realize that God was there the whole way through and was trying to show me the path, but I was refusing to travel down it. My struggle was creating a constant internal conflict. I see similarities between me not having a relationship with my father and resisting a relationship with my heavenly father. Not having my father in my life left me lacking in confidence and missing fatherly love, making it more difficult for my heavenly father to have an influence in my life.

I want to make it clear; I still struggle today, but I accept God in my life again. I don't have all the answers, but I know that my growing love for God coincides with my growing love for myself. I no longer have anxiety because I know God has always been there to protect me. My struggles throughout my life were tests of strength, and I made it through them all. The scared boy of long ago was fatherless, but today I accept my heavenly father. The tough lessons that I experienced and my lack of an earthly father have been a great motivating factor to be an even better father for my son.

I think about how common it is for people to ingest all types of powerful drugs to sedate themselves so that they don't experience pain. But it is essentially them trying to avoid God's call to strengthen their resolve. There is no success without struggle, and accepting God by your side doesn't take away the struggle but provides a comforting strength. Feeling pain is natural and we shouldn't hide from it. If I had to live it all over again, I wouldn't change anything because those moments of pain made me who I am today. Those moments of pain showed me I can withstand anything, and becoming fearless in life is the ultimate drug.

You think I didn't have the opportunity to take prescriptions for depression and anxiety? I chose not to because it felt unnatural. I chose therapy instead of sedation. I worked through my issues instead of remaining as a victim. I chose the hard work of reflection rather than throwing my hands in the air and blaming others for my issues. If you are able to accept responsibility, you become empowered because you are able to make the necessary changes.

I blame no one but myself and that strengthens, not weakens, me. It matters not what my father did or didn't do, because as a man, I am the master of my destiny. Failure or success, I can live happily knowing I have the freedom to decide how my life turns out. I know that no matter what decision I make; God will continue to be by my side.

Maybe you are someone who has had this battle with finding God in your life. I understand. You are not alone in this experience. Our world is becoming more secular, and it is leading to people finding gods in those who do not have their best interests in mind and following ideologues who care more about virtue signaling than actually living virtuously.

We are bending the knee for social causes instead of God's will. We cry out to be heard by our clearly flawed politicians. But we no longer care if or how God sees us. We want constant adulation regardless of the intention from those who are sending it in our direction. We'd rather find affirmation through a worthless "shout-out" to our race than shout out for God's grace. We have found new vices to worship, and this has left our religion-based moral tenants behind.

God hasn't left black America. Black America has left God. Many of us go through the motions of mentioning his name but don't truly believe in his moral principles. We find it hard to forgive, we are physically and materially gluttonous and we are skeptical when it comes to love. For many black Americans, love has been replaced with sexual gratification.

We no longer value marriage for its representation of God's love. And we have moved away from the belief that marriage allows two people to come together and potentially create loving offspring which can move our community closer to happiness. Now we encourage the creation of broken families that involve jaded parents and children who believe living in an environment of unbelief and chaos is normal.

Many of our modern black women refuse to be vulnerable with anyone, even God. They proclaim independence not only from men but from criticism, direction and compromise. No one dares highlight the level of arrogance that is ruining the mental state of many black women. If you do, they will make sure to respond with "You ain't my daddy". Truth is, even if you were their daddy, they wouldn't care because they have lost respect for men.

When independence resembles egotism, there is a problem. When one cannot question any behavior without facing hostility, we have a population of people who cannot be shamed. We tend to think of shame as inherently negative, but shame is appropriate in certain situations. We shame pedophilia because we universally see this activity as immoral. When we shame the immoral, then we show what is acceptable and that we will take a stand if you cross that line. Once the line is crossed, we all agree that punishment is necessary. Otherwise, dangerous behavior becomes socially acceptable.

The sexual revolution has convinced our black women that they have the choice to operate without shame and also without responsibility. She can choose one man for the rest of her life or hundreds of men because we are no longer allowed to shame her even when her behavior is self-destructive. We have taught these women that their sexual prospects determine her worth and feminism tells her that she can and should live as sexually free as a man.

How dare we shame a woman who wants to have multiple children with multiple undesirable men outside of marriage? How dare we point out that this is not good for her children's well-being? How dare we challenge the conceited belief that she can take the place of both parents in her children's lives? How dare we not accept your desire for multiple sexual partners in replacement of femininity?

Whether or not people want to say it out loud, being a whore is shameful (for men and women) and we shamed it in the past because we did not want sexual promiscuity to replace family responsibility. Anyone can be forgiven as long as they change their ways for the betterment of themselves, their children, and those that surround them.

Men like my father lack remorse when they leave their child's mother with all the burden as they wonder about the world. They too have been conditioned to feel no shame in this as they spread their seed around town but never truly help watch their seed grow. We used to have a moral obligation to be accountable for our actions, even if it wasn't a planned situation.

We used to teach our men to be careful about who they laid down with because you will be accountable for what comes from such an experience. Now, we expect so little from our men that we don't even blink an eye when this occurs because all the expectation has been laid at the feet of our black mothers. Today, if you were to ask a black person if their father was in their life, it is unlikely that they will say yes. What's even worse is realizing how many of us don't even know who our fathers are. These men can only exist in a community that no longer shames immoral actions.

When our boys become young men and get caught up in a life of violence, we indulge their victimhood instead of doing what their fathers should have done, shaming them into social obedience. We describe them as "set up for failure" indicating that we believe they had no choice but to fail and that they had no real agency over their actions. When we do this we coddle them rather than holding them accountable.

We consistently bail them out of their responsibility instead of allowing them to learn from their failures. We bail them out of jail when we know they are guilty. We bail them out of fatherhood so that they do not need to behave as a father. We bail them out of manhood when our black women become the masculine figure. We refuse to allow many of our black men to acknowledge their flaws and accept the consequences, so that they don't become wiser through suffering.

When our girls become young women without direction and they get caught up in a life of debauchery, we indulge their actions and even pay for their recklessness. When she makes the decision to procreate with an undesirable man, she has all the safety nets of the government to cover her indiscretion. We consistently bail women out from their failing decisions with court mandated child support, court mandated alimony, welfare and a variety of other government programs.

Without these resources either provided by or enforced by the state, women would need to be selective in their sexual relationships. As it is now, we all pay for it in the long run with increased taxation and the breakdown of our society.

Shaming these behaviors would lead to greater selectivity and better family choices. We live in a free society and if you want to destroy your body and soul, as long as it doesn't affect anyone else, have at it. The problem is that this sexual freedom comes at a price and causes other human beings to be born into dysfunction and a general societal decline.

"For if someone does not know how to manage his own household, how will he care for God's church?" – 1 Timothy 3:5

If our homes are broken, then we will not care for God's home. If we are children of God, God is our father. Our family is meant to be an extension of God's family. But if our family is broken, how do we properly relate to God? God is the essence of love, respect and honor. Who do we love, respect and honor within our own homes?

We are far too worried about autonomy and power dynamics within a home, but the conversation rarely turns to love. We always want, but we aren't willing to give. We want love unconditionally, but we place conditions on giving love. Women want children instead of a family. We see marriage as a restriction instead of a union. We don't trust even those that we claim to care about and this creates insecurity. We aren't willing to put in the work to make good families happen.

If you believe in God's will, how can you act as a victim? If you believe in God's will, then logically you should have faith that God has instilled enough willpower into you to overcome life's tribulations. To be a victim means you do not trust God's goodness and wisdom.

- CHAPTER 16 -

IGNORANCE AND HIP-HOP

"Is this it? This is what I got all those ass whoopings for? I had a dream once. It was a dream that little black boys and little black girls would drink from the river of prosperity, freed from the thirst of oppression. But lo and behold, some four decades later, what have I found but a bunch of trifling, shiftless, good-for-nothing niggas? And I know some of you don't want to hear me say that word. It's the ugliest word in the English language, but that's what I see now: niggas. And you don't want to be a nigga, 'cause niggas are living contradictions! Niggas are full of unfulfilled ambitions! Niggas wax and wane; niggas love to complain! Niggas love to hear themselves talk but hate to explain! Niggas love being another man's judge and jury! Niggas procrastinate until it's time to worry! Niggas love to be late, niggas hate to hurry!"

– TV Show

"The Boondocks"

spoken by a fictionalized Martin Luther King Jr.

America has monetized black ignorance for entertainment. Within the black community, we used to avoid the ignorant and disparagingly referred to them as "niggas" because they always brought dysfunction along with them. They were people who loved living in filth as long as it was given to them by the government. They were the people who felt that working was for suckers. They were those who would cause drama for their own personal entertainment. They were full of pride as much as they were full of shit. They were strong in their opinions but couldn't explain how they came to their conclusions.

When we encountered them, we hoped that our interactions would be as short as possible, as if ignorance were air-born and we didn't want to catch what they had. We certainly didn't want to procreate with them because that would taint our bloodline. They were the undesirables within our community, and we had no interest in mimicking them.

They spoke differently than the rest of us as they proudly mispronounced the English language while having no regard for their volume. If you witnessed them in a majority white area, you prayed they could keep their ignorance to a minimum and hoped that no one would think you were related to them.

I am reminded of a comedy bit by Chris Rock during his 1996 stand-up special titled "Bring the Pain" where he was able to create humor around the people I am describing. This comedy bit is known as "Niggas vs. Black People" which highlights the divide within the black community at the time.

"Who's more racist? Black people or white people? Black people, you know why? Because we hate Black people too! Everything white people don't like about Black people, Black people REALLY don't like about Black people. There's some shit going on with Black people right now. There's a civil war going on with Black people, and there's two sides: there's Black people and there's niggas. The niggas have got to go. Every time Black people wanna have a good time, ignorant-ass niggas fuck it up. Can't do shit! Can't do shit without some ignorant-ass nigga fucking it up. Can't do nothing."

The ignorant are people who are embarrassingly entitled, believing that they deserve what they have not earned. If they don't get what they want, naturally, it's because they are black and not because of their ignorance. Their pigmentation is the crutch that they carry around with them in case they need to beat the idea of racism into the heads of others who refuse to cater to their ignorance. No one really took these people seriously until recently.

In August 2020, America was in the middle of one of the most contentious elections during the battle for the Presidency between Donald Trump and Joe Biden. Americans wanted to hear from their potential Presidents and ask tough questions to get down to who deserved to lead this great nation. Obviously, there is only one person who is qualified for this immense responsibility… rapper Cardi B.

"I of course want free Medicare. And this is why it's important to have free Medicare, because look what's happening right now. You see why we should have been have free Medicare for a long time. I, of course, think that we need free college education, that's second. And I want black people to stop getting killed, and no justice for it. I'm tired of it. I'm tired of it, I just want more stricter laws, that is fair to black citizens, and it's fair for cops too. If you kill somebody that doesn't have a weapon on them, you go to jail. You know what? If I kill somebody, I got to go to jail. You got to go to jail too."

A bewildered looking Joe Biden stares into the camera as she continues with her list of demands…

"Obviously, free college education, free Medicare, especially now that people are just getting sick left to right, left to right. And that's why I keep telling people, because sometimes people have problems in they community. They just wonder, for example, a lot of afterschool programs that I was growing up with, there's no afterschool programs a lot anymore, in my hood."

This publicity stunt to gain the youth vote on the part of the Democrat nominee proves the point that there is an elevation of ignorant people in American society. Cardi B, the same person who complains publicly about how much money is taken from her to pay for taxes, is now advocating for multiple free government programs for Americans. She is too ignorant to even contemplate where that money would come from to pay for all these programs, and the answer is from people like herself who earn millions of dollars a year.

We are all ignorant about something. For example, I know nothing about brain surgery. If someone were to ask me to speak at a conference on brain surgery, I would have to humbly decline because I am aware of my ignorance. Truly ignorant people always have something to say about everything, and they are keenly unaware of how disconnected they are from reality. Most people know where their lane is located and have no problem staying within it. Meanwhile ignorant people swerve from lane to lane, proudly landing on the sidewalk.

To be clear, my criticisms of the ignorant do not mean I am an elitist. I appreciate people of all intellectual levels, and my intelligence alone does not make me better than anyone else. But Americans have become afraid to criticize the chronically dumb because we are afraid of being called elitist or mean spirited. Within the black community, we have gone so far as to put the ignorant on a pedestal when they should be easily dismissed.

We believe now that because someone has a talent or notoriety of some sort, that they should be looked upon as an acceptable influence for the black community. The entertainment that we used to get from watching these people from a distance is now broadcast to the masses, making ignorance trendy and tolerable.

TV Shows like "Love and Hip Hop" where they display the buffoonery that we used to cringe at when we saw it in our neighborhoods is now represented as typical black behavior. The behavior of overly aggressive, rude, disrespectful black people is broadcasted nationwide becoming the mind-virus infecting American culture.

Decades ago, we put an emphasis on getting a proper education because the ignorant don't tend to succeed. But now the ignorant are part of popular culture. Their behavioral traits are mimicked by the youth of black America, leading them down the path of debauchery. The ignorant teach our girls to engage in whoredom, and our boys to chase conflict. The ignorant encourage us to referring to ourselves as bitches and niggas which lowers us to their level. The black youth of America desire to be like the ignorant when in reality, we need to disassociate ourselves from these types of people.

We believe we are simply code-switching when we use one dialect with white people and a different one with black people. But in reality we are embracing ignorance. The ignorant act, live and speak in a dysfunctional manner. Yet now we believe that words like "proper" are associated with whiteness. If you're acting properly, you are following societal rules. But for some of us that feels too safe and white in nature. If your lifestyle involves cleanliness and you present yourself as humbly put together you are seen as unremarkably boring and white in portrayal. If you speak properly, you are presumed to be "dog whistling" your association with white America.

"One of the reasons we're never going to be successful as a whole, because of other black people. And for some reason we are brainwashed to think, if you're not a thug or an idiot, you're not black enough. If you go to school, make good grades, speak intelligent, and don't break the law, you're not a good black person. And it's a dirty, dark secret."

– Charles Barkley during a CBS Philadelphia radio program "Afternoons with Anthony Gargano and Rob Ellis"

Embracing ignorance is akin to embracing failure. There are failures within black society, and those failures should be used as teaching lessons rather than as something to celebrate. It has become popular to mimic the failures of a few. We think that sagging our pants is just a style for the youth rather than understanding that they are imitating prison culture.

The popularization of prison culture is exacerbating the issue for our black youth who are highly impressionable and impulsive. The school to prison pipeline isn't just because of the failure of public schools. It is also a result of failing to discourage this pathway within our culture. Our youth are less likely to divert from a particular trend if it is presented as enthralling and a part of black culture. With the growing number of broken black families, where do we think our black youth are getting their cultural cues from? Hip-Hop.

My views on hip-hop have changed throughout the years, ranging from feeling that it is no big deal to now seeing it as a cry for help. When I was younger, I saw it much like a movie, and most of the artists who appeared ridiculous were just playing a part for the audience. People like violence, so they are going to portray someone who is violent. Artists like Freeway, Scarface and Rick Ross adopted their names from real and fictional gangsters to give the audience the portrayal of someone that is dangerous and taboo for a civil society. Music that is edgy is much like driving past a car wreck. You cannot help but pay attention. We wait for the next hyper-violent, sexually driven and drug use glorifying song that becomes our life's soundtrack.

Our life's soundtrack is composed by the ignorant or people who are using the mentality of the ignorant for financial gain. There are obviously hip-hop artists who steer away from glamorizing black ignorance and choose to have more of a message, even if it's a controversial message. The problem is that there are not nearly as many of these artists in the mainstream due to the overwhelming economic benefit of propping up the ignorant.

The niggas we used to avoid are now our favorite musicians who proudly proclaiming themselves as niggas, their friends as niggas and everyone that they appreciate as niggas. Many of them talk openly about their drug usage, not from a cautionary standpoint but from a sense of pride, and admit that they enjoy being hooked on a substance. Drugs are their medicine to keep them mentally sedated so that they continue in their bereft thought processes.

Ignorance has no wealth dividing line because ignorance is a mentality. The ignorant are all about short-term gains. In some ways, they live a life of survival and excess at the same time. The poorest of the ignorant barely have any money to their name but will find ways to have the latest version of material goods. The richest of the ignorant, like ones we see in the hip-hop world, live purely in excess as if their money is never ending. The rich-ignorant make sure that we are aware of how much money they have and what they spend it on. This type of reckless spending is modeled for our black youth as well, giving the illusion that life is all about the material and not about the substance.

It is not bad enough that there is a black association with this culture, which pushes black people to adopt, even partially, what hip-hop culture has to offer. But it is funded by some of the largest corporations in the world. That's right, black ignorance is now sponsored by corporate

America and continues to bring in profits from our internal destruction. Viacom, estimated to be worth over 12 billion dollars, owns television channels BET, MTV and VH1. Keep in mind, Viacom's ownership of VH1 makes them the financiers of your favorite hood-rat television series "Love & Hip Hop". iHeartMedia, the owner of Power 105 in New York City and many other Hip-Hop stations nationwide, is another billion-dollar corporation. 3 of the largest hip-hop music distributors are Sony Entertainment, Universal Music Group, and Apple; all multi-billion-dollar corporations. These are only a few of the players within the world of urban media and music distribution.

Black ignorance is well funded, profitable and highly consumed. Everyone has a stake in the growth of highly influential and entertaining ignorant black folks. Corporations aren't about charity or goodwill; they are about profits and the bottom line. They don't care if the messages portrayed within the music that they are financing contributes to the decay of black people (and white people) nationwide. They are perfectly fine with degrading depictions of women, acceptance of gun violence and excessive drug usage because it is black faces portraying the black experience.

It's the "chicken or the egg" scenario. Are black Americans becoming more ignorant because corporate America wants to push this type of messaging into the black community, or is corporate America financing and supplying more ignorant messaging because black people want it? If you follow the economic concept of supply & demand, then the answer is the latter. If you consider the power of media to manipulate a population of people to adopt new cultural standards and trends, then it could be the opposite. It is likely the case that both are true. We are eager to digest ignorance and corporate America is eager to sell it to us.

Why do we want to consume this negative messaging? It is because we believe that the black experience includes consistent negativity. If you have a victim mindset, you believe that someone is always out to get you because of your race. We are trained to assume the worst about people, including ourselves. We are encouraged to embrace negative behavioral patterns. We have normalized calling each other negative words like niggas, meaning, ignorant. We are fine with holding substandard expectations for each other and ourselves. Black culture today is filled with negativity, making ignorant messaging through hip-hop attractive. Misery loves company.

The situation gets worse when you realize that the depiction of black people that other races see, who do not have daily interactions with black people, is through the prism of hip-hop. Black Americans are about 13% of the population and about 60% of black people live in 10 states (based on Census data). This means that there are plenty of white Americans that have little to no real interactions with black people. Their understanding of what black people are behaviorally and culturally, unfortunately, comes from hip-hop music and other forms of urban entertainment. These sources often represent us as ignorant clowns who are impulsively sexual and violent. This poison that is fed to white America creates a false representation of all black people. It gives the appearance that degeneracy is in our DNA.

White Americans who enjoy hip-hop culture are presented with a false view that all of black society is inherently dangerous. This may be attractive to someone who lives with the luxury of constant safety. They believe they can live the black experience vicariously through hip-hop culture. They stop short of digging deeper into the reality that they are admiring the ignorant. Those who admire hip-hop culture use these stereotypes as measurements of blackness to determine who is legitimate within the black community. This leads them to associate anything that is positive, boring and safe as characteristic of whiteness and anything that is negative, excitingly reckless, and dangerous as characteristic of blackness.

The ignorant give lessons on identifying who or what is "authentically black". The ignorant believe their way of living is the most authentically black experience rather than seeing it as the outlier. There is a growing attitude of white empathy towards black Americans, even to the point of feeling the need to save black Americans. This view of all black Americans as being too ignorant to save themselves only validates the savior complex of many white leftists. They will fight harder for ideas like prison reform or bail reform because they only see black people as ignorantly criminal-minded people who just need a white helping hand.

Even the ignorantly rich black portrays themselves as the victim of a terrible society despite the fact that it gave them more wealth than the majority of the world. They are never satisfied with what they have achieved; not because they are ambitious but because they like to complain. They whine and moan about their alleged haters because they have been trained to express negativity since birth and subscribe to black pessimistic thought. What is ironic about their self portrayal as victims is that they also portray themselves as perpetrators of unlawful behaviors to garner more street credibility. The perpetrator lifestyle that they promote and celebrate only feeds into the negative stereotypes of black men, creating hostility and fear in reaction to our existence.

For white Americans who despise hip-hop culture, the constant imagery of black thuggery encourages a hostile reaction against the average black person. With little to no interaction with black Americans, they are unamused by the negative behavior that is glamorized. When they see anything that resembles hip-hop culture in the real world, for example, the type of clothing that someone wears, they assume that the individual who dresses that way subscribes to the behavior that is being promoted.

The most detrimental part of the growing influence of these ignorant black stars has been their influence over our children who like all teens are naturally somewhat rebellious and daringly edgy. The ignorant give our lost black boys a blueprint for manhood that they never received from their fathers. The ignorant show our boys how to garner respect by mimicking terrorists and felons. They present drug dealing as no big deal and hide the danger of this lifestyle to sell this message to our lost boys. When our lost boys need a void filled within their soul, the ignorant will point them in the direction of the nearest lost girl who is looking for the same.

The ignorant within Hip-Hop culture have taught our lost boys to treat their women like cars and their cars like women. They've taught our men that looking for love is for weak niggas. Strong niggas scavenge for pussy and discard once done. The ignorant have also taught our lost girls that being discarded by men is to be expected and to avoid being hurt, they should discard the men first. Our lost girls are taught that their relational appeal depends purely on their sex appeal, resulting in our young women defining their level of self-esteem through the prism of overt sexual appeal by wearing overtly sexual apparel.

Whether or not you realize it, the ignorant have gained favorable notoriety within black culture and they have even broken into mainstream American culture. They are being taken seriously, they are given millions, and corporations are clamoring for the next ignorant superstar that they can prop up. The culture of the ignorant has blended into black American culture, and if we do not realize this power, they will take over as the predominant influence makers.

- CHAPTER 17 -

SOLUTION - REUNIFYING THE BLACK FAMILY

As a child I used to play baseball for the local little league, a sport that I enjoyed despite not being the greatest player. I remember one of the best feelings was to have a great game and see our team mentioned in the local newspaper, which was a rarity for me. I always tried my best when playing baseball, and I took pride in what I could do, even if it was at a mediocre level.

Every season I had a coach who was the father of one of my teammates. I would look in the stands and see complete families smiling, cheering and celebrating the successes of their children on the field. Sometimes my mother would be in the crowd cheering me on. But my father was nowhere to be found. I was envious of my teammates who had a father who cared enough to show them the mechanics of swinging a bat, teach them to pitch like their favorite big-league player or just take the time to bond with them. It would become obvious that my white teammates' family dynamic involved two parents while mine did not.

My mother also had me involved in the Boy Scouts at a young age to help me be around male figures, and it was the same dynamic. Fathers standing side by side with their sons as scout leaders or seeing fathers come to pick up their boys after a fun scout meeting. These men in training had a male figure to model themselves after, whereas I would have to guess my way through manhood.

I remember wanting to ask them what it was like to have a father, but it always sounded like a ridiculous question to ask. Even if they could answer this question, I would never fully understand what it feels like to have a man love you unconditionally. There was nothing I could do to convince my father to even care about my existence. As much as I despise how my father neglected me throughout my life, I would be lying if I didn't wish that I could turn back time and have my father in the bleachers cheering me on when I was up to bat. I would give just about anything to have my father give me a hug and tell me he's proud of me. Even with such daydreams, I always have to wake up to the fact that those opportunities passed decades ago and the father that I dreamt of is metaphorically and literally dead.

The death of my father was the death of possibility for me. Years before his death, I had given up hope of reconciliation because both parties have to care to reconcile, but his death solidified the end of wondering if I would receive a phone call from him to apologize for his purposeful disappearance throughout my life. His death silenced my wishful desire for him to give me some type of lame excuse as to why he hadn't been a part of my life, so I can just move forward with the man I always wanted in my life. I didn't hate my father; I was just disappointed in him and that feeling remains even as he lies dead.

As a father now, I could never do what my father did to me. I could never leave my son wondering if his father loves him or if his father is proud of his accomplishments. When my son received an award for honor roll, I was there to tell him how proud of him I was. When he didn't believe in himself, I motivated him to live up to the expectations that I knew he could reach. When he wants to talk to his father, I always make myself available. I am not perfect, but no child requires a perfect father, just a father who is trying his best.

I know I am not alone in how I grew up, especially in the black community. Besides the obvious statistics about single-parent homes, meaning homes without fathers, I've met countless black men and women that have had similar situations to me. It's sad to say, but I can probably count on one hand the number of black men and women that I've met who grew up with both parents. This family disconnect leaves children like me emotionally handicapped throughout our lives.

The reunification of the black family is paramount to our long-term success. But it can only proceed with conscious decision making and purposeful procreation with suitable partners. Creating children without the solidifying effect of marriage and choosing sexual gratification without consideration of potential ramifications only continues the demise of what used to be the foundation of the black family.

This lifestyle that we've been living creates broken people, and they repeat the cycle with their offspring. We have to be mindful of the repercussions of our actions and we need to reexamine the importance of father involvement in the black family. The removal of the black father has hurt black women by giving them the singular burden to perform the impossible task of being everything for their children.

My mother worked tirelessly and struggled at times to provide the things we needed in addition to being the support system for us while growing up. B:ut there is nothing that she could have done to fill the emptiness that my father created within me. We are preaching to black women to be something that they are incapable of being and we downplay the importance a father plays in their child's life.

Black boys face an uphill battle to discover what healthy masculinity is without their most influential male role model. Black girls are also hindered in developing healthy male-to-female interaction which often leads them into the arms of broken men and potential predators.

Our children are the ones who pay for our poor decision making so we have to reconsider how we proceed. No one is perfect, but we can strive for better results as long as we acknowledge that this is in fact a problem. The lack of acknowledging this problem to satisfy ideological notions originating from feminism has selfishly uplifted women at the expense of our children.

As a child of a single mother, I can acknowledge that my mother did the best she could do by herself. But I also believe that my childhood was far from ideal and would be seen as abnormal outside of the black community. We can congratulate our mothers for their effort in raising us, but we can also advocate not repeating the same poor decisions that they made that put us in these broken situations.

The men are not to be let off the hook, including me. I put my son at risk of experiencing hardship similar to what I grew up with by having him out of wedlock and at a young age without secure economic support. I cannot change the past, but I can help mold his future. In order for me to do better, I had to acknowledge this danger I put my son in and work even harder to keep him from falling into the emotional depths of despair that I did as a child. Without acknowledging the problem, there cannot be change, and without change there cannot be prosperity in the black community.

Our broken black fathers must acknowledge their mistakes and their faults to become the men the black community needs. If you've made mistakes, understand that we all have, but sweeping them under the rug will only continue the pain for you and your children. Our black men must recognize their importance as providers of not just finances but of emotional support for their children. Our black men must rediscover their masculinity and reject the bastardization of masculinity within the black community. We must embrace stoicism in moments of conflict and be resolute when it involves our children.

For far too long, we have disregarded the tears and insecurity of children coming from single-parent homes. People like me have been ignored when we state how much this has affected us because it would highlight a significant flaw in the black community. We are voiceless as children and when we grow up, we are shouted down when we criticize certain behaviors within our community or shamed for appearing to wag our fingers at our strong black mothers.

When we advocate for masculine fathers, we are called sexist or patriarchal. But as a child I had never heard those words and yet the desire for a father figure persisted. The insinuation that those who advocate for a father in the home want to demonize women or be overtly pro-man to spite women only leads to the continued emotional pain among children in single parent homes. Reunifying the black family would cause our lost children to become found again.

In order to reunify we must as parents or potential parents be prepared to sacrifice for something greater than ourselves, our children. We need to regain the ability to compromise within our relationships because you can't always win. Our black women need to stop competing against black men and stop denigrating black men as a method of female empowerment because it only pushes men away in the long run. Our black women need to quit acting as if black men are replaceable objects or meaningless for their and their children's happiness while simultaneously using them for their procreation needs. Our black mothers need to remove the juvenile definition of fathers as "baby daddies" and help to foster an environment that allows men to return to the home as proper fathers.

Our black men need to stop doing the bare minimum of fatherly participation. You do not deserve congratulations for something you're supposed to be doing. And you do not deserve a pat on the back for being an active participant in your child's life. Our black men need to hold each other accountable for our actions or lack thereof and not accept each other's pitiful attempts to join in on our children's lives.

We need to stop making excuses for our lack of involvement because no matter how terrible the mother is, you owe it to your child to fight for your right to participate in their upbringing. Giving up should never be an option because you are ultimately giving up on a child who has no say in the matter and is stuck in the middle. Part of your job as a father is to speak on behalf of the child that is voiceless and to sacrifice your pride for the betterment of his or her future.

About 70% of black Americans grew up in this dysfunctional dynamic, and we have a lot of traumas because of it. I know I am not alone in my feelings as a child of wanting my father to acknowledge my existence. I know that life is complicated, but we sometimes increase the complication unnecessarily or don't consider the emotions of others for whatever reason. My story is unfortunately not unusual in the black community, and that is the real tragedy.

Consider the life that you will create for your potential child before you engage in sex out of lust. If you were a lost child like myself, remember back to how you felt growing up in dysfunction and ask yourself if you want that to be the legacy you pass on to your child. Do you want to be a mother who chooses to ignore the emotional needs of your children and raise them alone so as to not have to share control? Do you want to be a father who chooses to disappear instead of demanding involvement? Does your child's emotional well-being matter more than your pride? If so, reunification is possible.

- CHAPTER 18 -

SOLUTION – ACCEPTANCE AND COMMONALITY

"You see, as a Christian who believes the Bible, I am very suspicious of the way we frame the whole discussion of race in the first place. I believe that all of us have come from the same parents and that we are all really one race, the human race. Thus, for example, when I speak to you I didn't think of you as another race. I think of you as a distant cousin who just looks different from me in some ways. We are both made in the image of God and have ultimately both come from Adam, who, for all I know, looked a lot more like you than me."

– Pastor Keith Throop

One of the most difficult skills that I had to develop was the ability to accept myself and others. When you spend years of your life doubting yourself and experiencing depression, you will struggle with self-acceptance because you don't like who you are. You will think others are judging you as well because if you are focused on your imperfections, everyone else must see them too. You will tend to walk with your head down rather than holding it up because you are not proud of what you have become.

The mental anguish that this victim mindset puts people through places so many hurdles in front of us, preventing us from reaching our true potential or seeing other people's potential. Even love from others will be placed under a microscope because why would anyone love a person who doesn't love himself?

Even when I did not accept myself because of my personal mental victimization, there was always one person who did: my Great Aunt Anne. I started going to my Aunt Anne's house during my adolescence and mainly for the holidays. If you were to meet my Aunt Anne, you would remember her for her laugh and smile. She didn't care who you were, she would greet you lovingly in her home. She was sharp-witted and had a great sense of humor. She would see a seemingly innocent situation and laugh at the absurdity that we all missed. She spoke up when she needed to and stayed quiet when it was necessary. She would never tolerate disrespect in her home, but she rarely had to flex her muscle because everyone respected her.

My grandmother died when I was very young, so I did not have my grandmother there to spoil me or give me grandmotherly love, but my Aunt Anne was in a way my grandmother figure. As a child, I wasn't very materialistic, so I did not want many things, like toys and video games. My Aunt Anne gave me exactly what I needed every time I saw her: love and acceptance.

This love and acceptability permeated throughout her own adult children who only cared that I was happy. My Aunt Anne's best friend was a neighbor who was white, but she might as well have been her sister. They cared for each other, respected each other and her friend was always there anytime my aunt needed something. I never had the impression that skin color mattered to my Aunt Anne, what mattered was character. The Aunt Anne I knew hugged every person who walked into her home no matter their race, gender or political beliefs. My Aunt Anne was the embodiment of love, and love doesn't give a damn about what you look like.

As I grew older into adulthood, my visits to her home grew less frequent due to work obligations and relationships. I still feel guilty about not being there as much to see her due to distance and being more involved with my own issues. But in my heart, I know she understands. When I would show up, she was just as happy to see me and treated me no differently. There were no guilt trips or shaming, just happiness to see each other.

As my visits grew less frequent, Aunt Anne's physical deterioration became more hauntingly clear to me. The Aunt Anne that I grew up with was gradually disappearing physically, but her mind was still intact. She always sat at the head of the table for Thanksgiving dinners, even if she had to have her oxygen tank next to her. Even in moments of suffering, she still laughed and smiled because her family's happiness and togetherness were more important to her than anything else.

One evening I received a call from my cousin stating that Aunt Anne was being placed in hospice care because there was nothing more that they could do for her. The doctors said it was only a matter of time before she would be gone. I knew I could not take this warning lightly, so the next day I drove frantically for over 3 hours to see her one last time. When I reached her home, she was asleep because of sedation so that she wouldn't have to suffer from the constant pain. So I waited.

Day went into the night, and my cousin told me she was awake. Fearfully I walked up the stairs and there lay my Aunt Anne in a hospital style bed. Fragile, disoriented and in pain, she lay there moaning in agony. I held her hand saying my name and telling her I'm here with her but who knows if this message went through. Her hands felt brittle and so was my heart watching my beautiful Aunt Anne suffering in front of me. I must shamefully admit that shortly after that experience, I drove home cowardly into the night. I was not prepared to see her in that state, and I knew she didn't have much longer on this earth with us.

The next morning my cousin called me tearfully, saying words I will never forget, "She's gone." It was like getting hit by a bus because I realized that I would never get to hug her or hear her laugh again. I tried to remain strong by going to work, but I broke down crying in my car in the parking lot. I tried holding it together to call my boss, but I broke down again on the phone with him. In the following days, I had to learn how to do something that I didn't want to do: accept her death.

In the days leading up to her funeral, my cousin asked me to be one of her pallbearers. I agreed with nervousness and honor. The day of her funeral was a struggle. I wanted to be outwardly strong, but I had to hold back my desperate cries. At her funeral I saw all the people that she had impacted positively, including family, friends and neighbors. I saw how her love had spread to people of all backgrounds because love doesn't discriminate.

The moment of truth had come as it was time for me to carry her casket. Nervously, I walked to her casket to bring her to her final resting place, holding back tears of sorrow. When I placed my hand on her casket, I felt something that I had never experienced before in such a sudden fashion - a sense of calm. It's extremely difficult to explain, but it was like someone put their hand on my shoulder and said, "Everything is going to be alright." From that moment on, I didn't cry anymore. I can't come up with any other explanation for that feeling other than it was my Great Aunt giving me one last hug to calm me down. She was no longer suffering, so I had no reason to suffer anymore either.

My Aunt Anne is the example that I try to live by. And she is the example that black America should live by. She accepted everyone for who they were and not what anyone said they should be. She loved everyone but would not tolerate disrespect or bad behavior. Black Americans need to accept all black people for who they are and not what they think they should be.

We tend to judge those that we do not understand rather than accepting them for who they are. Acceptance of others is not a weakness. It is a strength. The ability to accept those that look like you but think differently than you will allow you to expand your understanding of humanity. When we divide ourselves into different factions we tribalize ourselves and point fingers at each other. We create narratives and boxes that we try to fit others into.

We have to be able to accept our past for what it is and not clammer for a rewrite. If we are to live peacefully in a multi-racial and multi-ethnic society, we have to stop measuring ourselves against what we think others have that we don't. We have to be able to look inward for what we can control rather than trying to find reasons to be envious. The ability to accept ourselves and choose to be victors and not victims would be the greatest skill set that we could ever achieve.

We should expect the best of people and be prepared for the worst. Sadly, right now it feels like the opposite is true. Acceptance will shine a light on the humanity of people instead of hoping to expose a hidden demon.

It is hard to accept people lovingly when you believe you are superior to them. This could be said for some black Americans who use black supremacist rhetoric routinely. Acceptance and supremacy cannot co-exist. If black Americans are to live morally, we have to be able to accept white Americans, which means, giving them the benefit of the doubt rather than jumping to negative assertions. We need to get to the point where we truly see someone's character despite their complexion. This would indicate true individual acceptance.

We have always had more in common with our white brothers and sisters than what is consistently preached to us by people who want to make a buck based on our separation. As someone who has traveled a bit, I've learned that people of every culture generally want the same things. They want a strong community, they want safety for themselves and their family, and they are generally willing to do whatever it takes to achieve these things, including making sacrifices.

We all generally want the same things. How we approach them may be different depending on our culture. As Americans, we share many things in common with each other despite our racial differences. The greatest tragedies in American history have always revolved around convincing one group of powerless people that they should fear the other group of powerless people, all for the entertainment and control of the powerful puppet masters.

The issues that I mention through this book are targeted at the black community. But ask anyone from any other racial group. They all experience it. Black men aren't the only men stepping away from their family obligations. I've met white men who have done the same thing. Black women aren't the only ones who are selfishly creating children without regard to the father's involvement. I've met white women who have done the same. Black people aren't the only ones with broken homes. I have met many people from similar circumstances who were white.

As a black man in his mid-30s, I theoretically should have nothing in common with a white man in his 70s. Through the magic of the internet, I by chance met such a man named Phillip. A man who from a distance would look like my polar opposite. But the more we discussed life, the more we saw that we experienced life in similar ways, especially based on our childhoods.

He grew up without his father. As a matter of fact, he doesn't know who his father is. He spent most of his youth directionless and always surrounded by femininity while feeling insecure about his own masculinity. He struggled in high school much like myself, finding it difficult to concentrate or even take instructions seriously. With no idea of what he wanted to do with his life, he joined the Army which helped to give him the direction and purpose he was missing.

The emotional struggles that we both experienced as children affected us similarly as adults. We both had issues staying in one place. I moved from town to town and state to state. He moved from country to country. We both had issues finding a place to truly call home and lived semi-nomadic lives. Unfortunately for him, he turned to alcohol earlier in his life which would cause more turmoil than anything else.

We are different, but we are the same, and that's the beauty of humanity. The ability to find commonality with people who you think are not like you opens up doors you will be glad to walk through. We spent countless hours talking to each other about life, relationships, race and conservatism. We strove to find what we had in common and learned more about those things that were different between us.

In our conversations, we spoke to each other as Americans who want greatness for everyone. He cares about his family just as much as I care about my family. He wants economic opportunities for all Americans, including black Americans. He wants nothing but the best for people like myself as long as we want the best for our fellow countrymen and women.

Our conservatism brought us together, our childhood pain helped us listen to each other and our care for each other maintains our friendship. My relationship with Phillip has made me a better person and he would say the same thing. We can speak openly and honestly. If we had not sought to find commonality, we both would have lost out on a genuine connection.

Americans need to strive for common ground regardless of ways in which we may be different. You can sit in your tribe and feel good about yourself, but you will be sheltered away from other beautiful people who have a perspective on life that you could genuinely learn from. The puppet masters want us all divided because they fear the day that we can unite against their manipulation. If we discovered that we have more in common than is different, then the discussion of race within America would become a moot point. I can't wait for this day.

- CHAPTER 19 -

SOLUTION - FINDING PURPOSE AND GOD

THE PURPOSE COMPASS

Individual greatness throughout history has been because of someone finding a passion within themselves that causes them to excel. They find a purpose in their life, something that drives them to become greater than how they had previously seen themselves. Purpose gets you up in the morning, makes your heart beat for the next step and can unlock the potential that is within you. A lack of purpose leaves the body in a zombie-like state and gives off an aura of dreary contempt for yourself.

We all know someone who lacks purpose, who lacks drive and has given up on themselves. The extreme case would be someone who commits suicide because suicide is for those lacking passion who no longer see any hope for themselves. Many who do not go to this extreme wander around communities across this country looking for the next "thing" that will give them pleasure. But it is not fulfilling. Drug addicts mask their pain with destructive endorphin hits to the brain. But this pleasure is only temporary. Criminals find purpose in crime. But a life of crime destroys you and those around you. Crime is the outward manifestation of what the criminal feels inside - chaos.

A body without purpose is a body in chaos. Purpose tells you which direction to head like a compass for our lives. Those without purpose feel as though they have a magnet sitting on top of their compass, causing it to spin aimlessly in any direction.

In black communities around the country, we see the despair in people's eyes as they struggle to believe they have a purpose in this world. Why are they here? What is the purpose of their existence? We see children in the streets taking up gang culture because gangs provide a purpose, even if it is to their own detriment. We see miserable people shuffling their way through impoverished streets without an idea of where they are going and why they are going there. The most chaotic cities are falling apart just like the people who live there.

When you see the popularization of street culture, you are viewing the romanticizing of a purposeless lifestyle. A man with purpose is not trying to steal from his neighbor, as he is too busy being passionate about something that matters. A man with purpose does not need to kill over territory or to protect his pride because purpose occupies his mental landscape. A man with purpose does not need to use women for pleasurable escapism. Purpose is far more pleasurable and fulfilling. A man with purpose does not need to use narcotics to block out life because life is worth experiencing.

The correlation between the lack of fathers and the lack of purpose is undeniable. Once again, this is not to say that mothers do not play a role or that they lack importance. But children view their father as their family's compass to guide their behavior. If the father provides the proper direction, the children are far likelier to succeed. If the father is purposeless and lacks a functional compass, the children are likely to reflect a similar attitude and may find themselves taking the wrong direction in life. If the father is not even present, the child will suffer and have no sense of direction.

Communities are nothing but groups of families, and if the families are broken, the community is broken. If the families lack a purpose, the community does as well. If we normalize meandering behavior in our black communities, we will become the underclass of black zombies looking for short term reckless pleasure rather than long term driven purpose.

We must ask ourselves, what is driving our communities? What is our place in American society? Are we just another cog in the wheel? I wholeheartedly believe that we can become just as successful as any other group of people. We know there is passion within our communities, but we need more people to help guide that passion. We know there is a flame that can be lit within the children in black communities. But we must ensure that the flame will not burn out due to a sense of defeat.

There is a clear lack of purpose but I am optimistic that we can fill this void. It is not so much a question of if we can fill this void, but do we want to fill this void? Will we redefine the concept of "hustle" to include meaningful positive activities rather than risky street behavior? Will we promote those who are successful to encourage excellence without poisoning it with racial classification? Will we remain in the darkness of demoralization or will we shine a light on the potential to overcome? I believe that we can move from being victims to becoming victors. When we clear away the dirt covering our paths, we will find the diamonds that have always been there.

THE RETURN OF GOD

This is not about the resurrection of Christ on earth, but more of a resurrection of Christ in our hearts. The black church held ground within the black community as a place of purpose for black Americans throughout the decades. The scripture served as a compass for the black soul, even when the path to redemption appeared foggy. The Bible was our book of hope and a guiding light to personal prosperity on earth and in the afterlife. The church served as God's home for his children and as a sanctuary from the craziness that often surrounded us.

As the years go by however, God is disappearing from black America. God was the Father that did not let you down and always had a purpose for you. But increasingly we resent God in the same way we resent our earthly fathers. One can only conclude that we have given up hope that God will intercede in our personal struggles of faith in American society. I don't blame anyone for feeling defeated as they wait on their building's stoop for God to make some visible change in a community that is falling apart.

Imagine living in a neighborhood where you're surrounded by death and despair. Every year the victims of murder get younger and younger. Supermarkets are replaced with food pantries. And jail is becoming an inevitable destination. An objective person can understand how someone looking at this surrounding does not see God because they are living in hell.

We devalued the role that the father plays, much like how we devalued the role God plays in our souls. Some may feel like God has abandoned them and is letting them suffer. We desperately want God's love, but we are looking for love in all the wrong places. We are desiring material wealth over internal peace. We want a quick fix to happiness rather than the long road to lasting peace. We are willing to walk hand in hand with evil rather than waiting for God to help deliver us to our destination.

Our view of God is much like our view of the Government; we want handouts. Many of us assumed that prayer was all we had to do, and God would handle the rest. I now believe that God operates like how a real father does. A real father doesn't remove the obstacles, he helps you understand why there are obstacles in the first place and it is up to you to figure out how to maneuver around them. You will not wake up one day with all your problems gone because that is not the purpose of God. I now believe that one role that God plays is by occasionally testing you in order for you to see that you can withstand tribulations.

I learned that God has been there the whole time and was stepping in when he had to. I can look back at the times of true personal struggle and find those odd moments when something would happen for my betterment that was truly unexpected. It was moments when God gave me a hand so that I could keep going.

When we find value in God again, we will find value within ourselves again. God is a representation of self as we are built in his likeness. The degradation of the black soul in American society coincides with the lack of belief in God's word in our community. I believe if we can accept our heavenly father again, we will accept our earthly fathers again as well. Both fathers provide that compass that we all need, and we should not desire to live the life of the directionless anymore. I have no illusions about the difficulty with accepting a family member again, but the rewards at the end can be unmeasurable. Once God returns, so will our purpose.

- CHAPTER 20 -

SOLUTION - STOP OVERLOOKING BLACK CRIME

If we are going to discuss human interaction in the context of race, then let's be fair in how we do it. If we can analyze and criticize white people, then it is only fair that we do the same for black people. If we are fair when we discuss challenging racial situations this could lead to a positive change for all Americans.

We must not only be fair, but also proportionate with our criticisms. This has always been a crucial flaw when black people talk about a myriad of topics that involve race. We have taken extremely rare and unfortunate situations that are complex, filtered them through a biased media apparatus and then exaggerated as being indicative of the "black experience".

The black experience is not monolithic. It is extremely varied depending on your economic status, your family structure, your age, your occupation, where you live and your personal philosophy. With all of these variables, we should realize that there is no such thing as the black experience. Instead, race should be seen as simply one aspect of the human experience. Rich black people aren't being murdered daily, the poor and lower-middle class are.

We have heard all of the old racial oppression tropes. Like being pulled over in a nice car simply because you are black in a white neighborhood. We act like this is something that we have all gone through, but the irony is that this could only happen to someone of a particular economic class. We have painted a picture of constant racial victimization by our supposed white oppressors for one major reason. We want to avoid the painfully obvious problems that exist in our own communities.

We must regain our humility and accept that we are not perfect because no one is. Individuals make mistakes all the time. And when many imperfect individuals make up a group the problems are multiplied. When the majority of the group subscribes to a particularly unhealthy way of thinking about themselves or engages in particular negative behaviors problems will arise.

Avoiding a discussion of certain aspects of black culture has led to overlooking black crime. Let us be fair. If we have no problem discussing crime when it involves any other racial group, then we have to speak about crimes committed by blacks in the same manner. If your initial reaction is to bring up things that other races do, this reaction is part of the problem. If you cannot hold those in your own tribe accountable to behave in certain ways, then why do you expect people outside the tribe to live more righteously than you? The solution is to lead by example.

If you see that there are issues within your community, you might work to get rid of these issues by changing the culture of your community. When crime increases in a town that didn't have crime before, what do people do? They rally together, start neighborhood watches, and they all take accountability for the community that they live in. They acknowledge that there is a problem and to battle against it they come up with plans, processes and increased awareness to attempt to slow down the criminal activity. When their community looks like it's unraveling, people take the initiative to revert back to their previous ways of living. They take action to help preserve the cultural standards within a community because without standards, then everything falls apart.

There is something wrong in our culture and our refusal to even acknowledge it has only furthered our own demise. When race suddenly becomes irrelevant to you because it's a black face committing an injustice, you are part of the problem. Mainstream black culture has accepted black crime as normal when we need to reject this type of behavior. We even go as far as romanticizing criminality, which is the sign of a downtrodden culture.

The "hood" is what we make it, not the inverse. If your neighborhood is falling apart, ask yourself, what can you do to help restore it? Rome wasn't built in a day and community restoration doesn't happen nearly as quickly as you may want it to. It takes brave men and women that are willing to sacrifice their livelihoods, reputation and dare I say safety to help restore what was lost.

Overlooking black crime only creates more black victims in the process. If people are going to violate the liberties of others, it is more likely that it will happen to someone within their own community. Where black crime is prolific, black suffering is abundant. The next time you avoid driving through the ghetto, understand that there are innocent black people that live there suffering the wrath of their local terrorists.

If we want genuine change, we have to be honest about what is going on. Fight for injustices but be proportionate with your outrage. If you care more when the perpetrator doesn't look like you, then you are not an agent for change, you are an agent for the status quo. If when you look at

261

prison cells filled with black bodies as 21st century slavery, then you are empathizing with tyrants while ignoring the people that they may have poisoned with drugs or violated violently.

Changing the culture helps to change our situation however ignoring our faults hurts black people economically, morally, and literally. We need to stop stepping over the graves of innocent black people that routinely die as a cost of living amongst terror. We need to stop chalking the death of our young black men as being casualties of war when there shouldn't be a war occurring in the first place. We need to stop cowardly overlooking and begin to bravely look the problem dead in the eyes if we want an actual change in our country.

- CHAPTER 21 -

SOLUTION - QUESTION THE LEFTIST AGENDA

"Moral principles do not depend on a majority vote. Wrong is wrong, even if everybody is wrong. Right is right, even if nobody is right."

—Fulton J. Sheen

In earlier chapters I referenced conservatism and its focus on individualism in hopes that you might consider a perspective that is not fairly explained in the mainstream media or culture. This book is not about converting you to one particular ideological platform, nor about getting you to switch your party affiliation. The purpose of mentioning conservatism is to give you another perspective to consider.

As a former leftist, I understand the positive aspects of this ideology, or at least the intentions behind it. Believe it or not, I believe we need those on the left as a healthy counterbalance for conservatism because too much of a singular ideology can be detrimental. The vast majority of black Americans vote along Democrat party lines and never consider what the other side offers or fully understand the Republican platform. This way of approaching politics has only contributed to our monolithic way of thinking.

To be clear, I am not a Republican. I view myself as an Independent and I believe Americans have been trained to marry a political party. Yet many of the politicians on both sides are politically and morally corrupt. If the political establishment is guaranteed your vote, they will ultimately do nothing for you. We are now treating average politicians as God-like figures waiting for their newest dogma when they are supposed to be serving us. When you are waiting for your moral cues from power hungry political egomaniacs, you are falling into a trap.

I believe black Americans need to ask critical questions before deciding what social and political policies they want to advocate for. I believe many of us practice "headline politics", meaning we see the title of a policy and listen to the surface level benefits but never read further into it. We have to question everything and compare it with our moral values before we endorse anything.

If you care about black people dying, then you should also care about the hundreds of thousands of black babies that are killed in the name of a woman's right to choose. If you are a believer in God, do you believe that it agrees with your moral principles to make every woman the judge and executioner over every pregnancy? Democrats tend to be against the practice of the death penalty because of its inhumanity. But wouldn't this be a conflict in moral judgment if you are a believer in the death of the truly innocent in the womb?

Leftists are big proponents of finding a pathway to citizenship for illegal immigrants who are here already and of defunding government border protection services like I.C.E. and U.S. Border and Customs. However, I.C.E. arrests thousands of human traffickers a year to help combat a growing problem at the southern U.S. Border. The breakdown at the border will lead to more human suffering as a result. These are people who believe that they are being brought to this country for a better life but who end up being sold into slavery. This results in women being raped repeatedly and children being molested. Are we willing to ignore the reality of human trafficking just to satisfy our emotional desire to appear as if we are helping people? How does this match up to your morals? Is the pathway to citizenship fair to those that followed the legal process to enter this country?

Many of the policies that leftists advocate for like universal healthcare, free 4-year college and paying off people's college debt for them all involve increasing the power of our government and giving them the authority to take more money from the average American. The government doesn't make money; it takes money and redistributes it. So, you have to ask yourself if you trust the people in charge enough not to squander your hard-earned money.

Many Americans believe the federal government is corrupt. Yet they want to give them more money, which would increase the amount of influence they have over us. The explanation given as to how we will pay for such large government programs is extreme taxation of the rich, but realistically, the wealthy elite in America have many ways of avoiding such taxation which will ultimately leave the rest of us to foot the bill. Are you alright with increased taxation that allows for funneling money to corrupt politicians? Is theft by extreme taxation a thievery that you are fine with? Is it morally right to take someone else's money to pay for another person's mistake? Should we agree to pay tens or hundreds of thousands of dollars for another person's regretful college experience?

Democrats are who black Americans overwhelmingly vote for, but what are black people getting for their vote? Places like Detroit, Chicago, Baltimore, New York City, Cleveland, Los Angeles County, and

265

Rochester have been primarily run by Democrats and they've been letting the same black neighborhoods drown while the local political elite swim beautifully. Cities like Baltimore are overwhelmingly run by black people within government, yet nothing changes for the better for their black residents. What are black people gaining from this deal? Does the Democrat political elite have a vested interest in keeping the status quo of substandard living within black neighborhoods? Is it moral to continually elect obviously corrupt politicians who steal resources from the poor to line their pockets?

These are also cities that receive the highest amount of funding per pupil within their states, yet continually produce poor results within their public schools. Democrats have demonized the idea of charter schools within black neighborhoods to keep the failing government monopoly on education in the poorest neighborhoods. These politicians are overwhelmingly supported by teachers' unions, and they would rather secure a job regardless of results than secure a future for black children in the most need. Is it moral to deny the possibility of garnering an education that could be the steppingstone to upward economic mobility? Is it moral to let innocent children remain educationally impaired as a sacrifice to political favors by unions?

As these children fail in school, many make their way to the streets where urban terrorism lives. Within these cities, gun crime increases, resulting in more despair for the average resident. The more danger that is present, the harsher the gun control measures are. In a city like Chicago, it is illegal to buy a gun within the city limits. The expense of buying permits, attending safety courses and the additional bureaucracy surrounding gun ownership for people who are living check to check leaves them vulnerable to the people who don't care about laws because they are criminals. Democrats want more restrictions for gun ownership, especially within larger cities, making it more difficult for people to protect themselves in the most dangerous of neighborhoods. Are gun restrictions working in these places when gun crimes are staying steady? Are we locking up people who are innocent but can't afford the lengthy process to legally own a gun? Is it moral to prevent people from being able to protect themselves from terrorists within their own neighborhood?

I believe these questions are valid to ask yourself before making social and political decisions. The more you can question policies and the moves of the collective, the more you can discern between what is morally right and wrong. If you believe in God or have some religious basis for your personal morality, then it's even more imperative to find a way to live your life according to what you believe regardless of tribal expectations.

Culture changes constantly, however your principles should remain relatively solid. If your principles change frequently, then it is likely that it's not you who is changing them, it's the collective. Holding onto sound principles, no matter the basis of these principles, is critical to preventing yourself from being manipulated by those that don't have your best interests in mind. Sound principles keep you from traveling along the path of the morally bankrupt. A man or woman without principles is a person without a solid moral foundation who is easily swayed by the narrative of the collective.

Questioning yourself is essential to experiencing personal growth in your life. Questioning yourself requires a level of humility because it shows that you are not infallible. Humility opens the door to receiving new perspectives that you may have never considered. Arrogance keeps the door shut so that you cannot experience the beauty of new ideas and the possibility of being wonderfully wrong about the world around you.

I don't have all the answers, no one does, however it is important to seek answers rather than swallowing what you are told without question. You may agree with all the leftist policies that I have described, which is absolutely fine. The point is not to have you switch your perspective. It is to have you question your perspective and make sure it matches your morals. Are you being principled in your beliefs, and does it match how you live your life? Are you being principled with what you support at the ballot box? Are the people or political parties that you support becoming your God or is God still your guiding light? Lastly, is a political agenda more important than your personal interests?

– CHAPTER 22 –

SOLUTION – ACCEPTING PEACE OVER CONFLICT

"Darkness cannot drive out darkness; only light can do that. Hate cannot drive out hate; only love can do that."

—Martin Luther King Jr.

Throughout this book I have detailed the experience of many black Americans that are dealing with either an internal or external crisis. They are conflicted in their approach to resolution for themselves, their families and their world around them. It is essential that we move forward with plausible solutions rather than fantastical concepts.

We are hopelessly in love with conflict because peace appears impossible. Why are we afraid to accept peace over conflict? Why would we rather see the worst in people than believe in the possibility of a misunderstanding? Why would we rather jump to negative conclusions than work toward possible peace? Why have we become a people of conflict when we were on our way to victory through peace? Is conflict our way of staying victimized and relinquishing responsibility to others?

We all know people who are frustrated with their existence and so they create conflict when there was none there in the first place. The modern black experience is one of being frustrated with our current situation and not understanding how we got where we are. When we attempt to investigate the source of our problems, we are constantly misled to believe that our entire existence has been one of subjugation and servitude to white America. We are told that our problems of today are entirely based on the slavery from the past, as if nothing has changed.

We remain a people in conflict because we have leaders that find us more controllable as conflicted people than as connected people. Politicians find us more compliant when we are in a state of conflict because we can only put-up minimal effort against their attempts to manipulate us. They treat us as a monolithic voting block and try to get us to lift them into power, even when we have little strength of our own.

The black elite want us in a state of conflict so that we will view them as our default leaders. They want us to believe that we are the only racial demographic that needs leadership because they don't believe we can lead ourselves individually. Conflict has become our continual state of being because we have spent decades absorbing negative victim rhetoric. And now we have been manipulated into becoming permanently conflicted so that we need others to take care of us.

War is detrimental to the people that are being attacked, but it can also be profitable for those that are supplying the weaponry for such a war. Peace is rarely profitable, which is why most organizations that are focused on peace require donations to stay in existence. Much like modern day warfare becoming a well-oiled machine that generates dollars and victims, American racial warfare does the same. No one wants to slow down the machine that crushes the hopes of black people, that manufactures black

270

victims for future manipulation, and that vilifies people like me that point it out. People like Al Sharpton are the arms dealers that are sponsored by corporations like Walmart, McDonald's and Coca-Cola to keep the racial war as the status quo.

They are not interested in creating jobs in black communities, creating community centers for black families, running after-school programs, promoting the nuclear family, providing affordable daycare centers, eradicating black genocide through abortion or anything else that could be seen as useful for black Americans because that would be the beginning of the end for their race profiteering.

In order to move forward, we must reject ideologies that have you look outward to find your oppressor rather than have you look inward to locate your victor. We must cast aside the desire for conflict and embrace peace as a possibility. We must rebuild our ability to find similarities between racial groups rather than highlighting our differences. We must ignore the media when they attempt to keep us in a position of conflicted weakness with false narratives. And we must question their motives when they make incredible claims of racism or racial bias.

In order to find peace again, we must understand how to love again. With love comes forgiveness and understanding - even with those that you adamantly disagree with. In order to find peace, you have to find a common ground with those that you believe are different from you because similarities are what brings us together. If black people are going to move forward in America, there has to be an effort to forgive.

Black men and black women have to be able to look at each other and forgive any wrongdoings that we have inflicted upon each other. Black people have to find a way to forgive America for its sins because the

America of yesterday is not the America of today. White Americans have to be able to forgive black Americans for our hypersensitivity to possible racial conflict and understand that it comes from a place of constant highlighted historical pain. Even more so, all of us have to be able to forgive ourselves for our part in the racial conflict.

In my life when I felt lost, I briefly gravitated towards "pro-black" rhetoric to allegedly find myself. This led me to assume there were negative motives within the white people around me. Eventually I realized that if I look hard enough for oppression anywhere, I will find it. I had to learn to forgive myself for possibly treating others differently because I assumed their intention based on their skin color or based on their political beliefs. The discovery of forgiveness within my heart has also allowed me to forgive people who are close to me that are flawed but well-intentioned. Forgiveness is the necessary road that we must travel on to reach our peaceful destination.

Forgiveness does not mean that you forget or excuse. Forgiveness enables the individual to stop feeling hatred and to stop allowing negativity to hold real estate in their minds. Forgiveness is not for the oppressor. It is for the victim to stop feeling victimized. Forgiveness is the method of releasing the internal hatred that has enveloped you in emotional pain. Forgiveness allows the individual to heal the soul and love again, regardless of differences or circumstances. Forgiveness is not so that you can forget the pain but so that you can remember the love.

Black people can remember slavery, lynchings, experimentations on blacks, segregation and a plethora of other wrongs that were directed specifically towards black Americans. But we have to be able to forgive at the same time. We have to be able to forgive the worst to become our best. Remembering the wrongs of the past can help us appreciate the present. When we confuse the present day with days of historical oppression, we are eliminating the possibility of forgiveness. We will thus remain paranoid believing that our oppressor still roams among us. Our forgiveness is a virtue, not a weakness. Our forgiveness is a strength of personal determination and not an attempt to be passive about our racial past.

Once forgiveness is achieved, we can start to embrace peace in our daily lives. Once we have peace in our hearts, love can flourish between all factions of American society. Love allows us to view each other as children of a God who can overlook race, political affiliation, and gender to see each other's humanity. As much as this makes me sound like some sort of Utopian hippie, I believe we can do far better than that state we are currently living in.

I have embraced peace because conflict only tore me down even further. After years of trying to understand why my life was always chaotic, I had to realize that internally I had no true peace. Anxiety and doubt are emotions that are exhibited when we are conflicted within ourselves, which is much of the emotion that I dealt with in my life. I doubted that there was a resolution for my victimhood as a child of a fatherless home and as someone who felt discarded by society multiple times when we were homeless. Anxiety filled my head to the point of creating a state of depression that would question my worth and whether I deserved love.

Individually we can have peace within ourselves and become examples for others as we work on the arduous task of overcoming victimhood. One by one we can make black culture return to the culture of yesteryear, in which we stood with our heads high in a peaceful manner, rather than cocked to the side with a scowl.

- CHAPTER 23 -

SOLUTION - EMBRACE INDIVIDUALISM AND DEMOTE GROUP IDENTITY

ho are you? How do you want to be seen in this world? How would you feel if I could tell everything about you based on what you looked like?

That last question is the question that really sticks with me when I think about black Americans. Based purely on statistics, I can look at a black person and be correct the majority of the time about their political party affiliation being in line with the Democrats, that they grew up in a single parent home, that they listen to Hip-Hop and/or R&B depending on their age and sex and I can even make a good guess at the state that they grew up in as 60% of black Americans live in 10 states.

Much about our lives is incredibly predictable, and this revolves around our consistent need to conform to group-think. But I ask again, who are you? Do you want to be seen simply as a person of a certain race or do you want to be seen as an individual capable of deciding your fate in this world?

There is nothing wrong with identifying as black, that's your prerogative. However, the problem arises when you never deviate from this identity to find your own identity. I know I am black, but that is not only who I am.

Sure; I listen to Hip-Hop music, but I also listen to a variety of music because it sounds good to me. Too many of us are sealed in this black identity box and are unwilling to leave it for fear of never being able to get back inside it.

Be an individual. Be who you want to be regardless of whether it makes you look like a nerd, uncool or dare I say "white". This world is filled with amazing things, and if you don't venture outside your box every so often, you are depriving yourself of potentially life-changing experiences.

Individualism allows you to be truly free in this world and follow your own path. There are those that will shame you along the way because you took a step outside the box, but that is because they are too scared to attempt it themselves.

Ignore the shaming. Ignore the condemnation. Ignore it all. Be an individual who is secure in yourself and find happiness wherever you may discover it. Open your heart to discovering ideas and meeting new people who have something special which you could bond with.

Demote your group identity… a bit. Become a person who happens to be black instead of a black person. Allow yourself to be somewhat unpredictable when people try to guess who you are. Surprise the world around you with how amazing you are because I'm willing to bet those amazing traits have little to do with your blackness.

Lower your guard and embrace love. Find someone that is the polar opposite of yourself and learn something from them. Open your mind to the possibility of being someone who is unique instead of common. Be daring enough to be wrong about people you don't know. It is perfectly fine to step over those cultural boundaries every so often to expand your wings, and if someone tells you otherwise, they are trying to prevent you from flying.

Be an individual. Be yourself.

- CHAPTER 24 -

SOLUTION - RESPONSIBILITY AND ACCOUNTABILITY

"Why have we had such a decline in moral climate? I submit to you that a major factor has been a change in the philosophy which has been dominant, a change from belief in individual responsibility to belief in social responsibility. If you adopt the view that a man is not responsible for his own behavior, that somehow society is responsible, why should he seek to make his behavior good?"

—Milton Friedman

O ne of the most difficult life exercises that I began years ago was accepting responsibility for my actions with no excuses added. I realized that many of my shortcomings in life were of my own doing. I had many moments when I felt helpless about my situation or helpless about someone else's decisions to not put the blame on myself. If someone else is to blame, then no responsibility is needed on my part.

I had reached a point in my life that was pivotal to my life trajectory. I had just moved back into my mother's apartment after another failed relationship at the age of 31. I was making a moderate amount of money but not enough to be truly independent and every night I went to bed alone suffering with my thoughts about my perpetual life failures.

Riddled with social anxiety and periods of depression, I was used to not taking responsibility for my emotional state. This irresponsibility had moved into the real world with regard to my personal relationships. I had the thought process that someone "made" me behave in a certain fashion rather than seeing it as myself deciding to allow someone else to sway my emotional state. Sometimes in my life I blamed God and even questioned his existence as I struggled with existing in such a harsh reality.

I had been in therapy for several years to help me cope with whatever situation that was at hand. But just trying to cope is a short-term solution. I was dealing with the pain from life beating down on me, but I didn't know how to stop it. I avoided the word responsibility when referencing myself and my actions in life.

I had lost who I was, what I was interested in, and my long-term goals during my latest relationship but not due to her but due to myself. I had gained nearly 50 pounds in a year, so not only did I not recognize myself internally but also in the mirror. I had fallen apart, and no woman wants to stay with a broken man. If you were to ask me at that moment what a man was, I don't know if I could answer that question for you because I was clearly not living up to my standards of manhood.

After the breakup, I had begged repeatedly to have her take me back, which ultimately became futile. After the anger and resentment left, I was once again depressingly alone. When you are depressed and alone, you have two options. Option 1 is to fall deeper into the victim mindset and do nothing about it. Option 2 is to pick yourself up and make a change for yourself. I had reached a point of being tired of falling asleep crying, tired of paying for therapy, tired of not knowing who I was and tired of not being a real man.

Sitting in my room alone allowed me to question myself and explore what I truly desired in life. It was then that I decided to work toward what I had always wanted to do and yet had always made excuses as to why I couldn't achieve it. It was in my room alone that I planned to travel to Europe, learn a second language and find a higher paying job to further my career. I was tired of letting life dictate what I achieved rather than dictating the achievements of my life. I had accidentally stumbled upon the first steps of personal responsibility and I was determined to try my hardest to reach these goals. I realized that if I failed at reaching these goals, it would only be my fault.

Looking ahead to today, my career has skyrocketed, rewarding me economically. I have been to nine countries (most of them alone) and I can have a decent conversation in German. None of this would have been possible if I didn't take responsibility for my own failures and learn to correct them to move forward in life. I decided to stop staying still, hoping that life will feel sorry for me long enough to have moderate success. My failures as a boyfriend in multiple relationships required me to take ownership to become a potentially successful husband. As of this writing, I am happily engaged to the perfect woman for me and the woman I finally deserve.

The great thing about taking personal responsibility is not just realizing that if you fail it's your fault. But also realizing that even if you fail, you're the one in control and you're the one who can change the outcome. I have failed multiple times in my life, ranging from poor relationships to homelessness, and if I could do it over again, I wouldn't change anything. It has been these failures that have allowed me to understand how strong I am to overcome rather than feeling like a helpless victim. I believe that we all need some form of failure to humble us and realign our thinking.

Success and failure go hand in hand and aren't mutually exclusive. I would even go as far as saying that I failed at the right times and the right number of times. I needed to experience not knowing where I would sleep to appreciate having a home. I needed to experience terrible relationships to appreciate a good relationship. I needed to experience these failures so I could be an even more effective father for my son.

Accepting personal responsibility means the death of victimhood. It requires us to take greater personal control, but it yields back a significant amount of power and success. Victimhood only holds you back. It prevents you from fixing your flaws because you perceive them as being caused by someone else. Once you have contracted the mind-virus of victimhood, it becomes pervasive in all aspects of your life. You become overtly victim-biased, feeling sympathy with other people's bad behavioral patterns. And you are more inclined to excuse the inexcusable.

Too many of us look at people who are in moderate distress as victims who need help rather than someone who needs to experience a momentary crisis to become more resilient. We have become enamored with identifying victims to the point of removing their responsibility for their individual outcomes. When my eyes opened up to my new belief in personal responsibility, I began to realize that western culture and black culture in particular has its eyes willingly closed.

We can certainly show sympathy for someone's personal experience, but that does not exclude them from being accountable for their actions. There is no need to feel sorry for someone who is an adult who willingly does something that results in an undesirable outcome. Many of us have unfortunate childhoods but this is not an excuse for being a terrible adult. When we become adults, it is our responsibility to change our situation no matter how far behind we may have started in the race. When you remove someone's accountability, you remove their power to change and you subjugate them to a status of permanent inability.

We need to reintroduce responsibility and accountability as priorities in black culture. The removal of responsibility has put black Americans in a place where they are always seen as victims of circumstance, even when they have created the circumstance themselves. White leftists see us as unfortunate creatures of an unfortunate past who need guidance rather than allowing us to grow from our historical misfortune. Black leftists also reject personal responsibility but, in this case, it is for their own benefit to garner empathy when necessary.

Situations that I experienced as a child do play a role in my life. But they do not determine my outcome. I am responsible for my actions as an adult. Blaming aspects of the past that are unchangeable only perpetuates the problem. When black people use historical excuses to explain the actions of present-day blacks, they are removing their responsibility and taking away their power to change.

Poverty is also not an excuse to commit crimes or act immorally. Those that choose to act in this manner are doing it of their own freewill. There are a plethora of options for people to take, but if you are a victim, you only see one. Economic poverty, especially in America, can be temporary as long as you're not suffering from mental poverty.

Slavery is not the reason our young black men are locked up, and neither is racism. Everyone makes a choice, even if it's a terrible choice. Many of these men grew up with broken black fathers that were much like my father, non-existent. Yet they are still responsible for their actions that led them into incarceration. When you excuse their behavior to make some false equivalency to slavery from the 1800s, you're robbing these men of the possibility of changing their life for the better and you're keeping them as society's victims. Post-slavery, the percentage of black incarceration was in lockstep with the black population, even during a time of legalized racial discrimination. Yet now we choose to make this association?

When you make excuses for other people you claim to care about, you're doing it for selfish reasons. It might make you feel better to believe that racism is the reason for all failures committed by black people rather than seeing it as an incredibly complex individual and cultural issue. The claims of constant racism as the mechanism for black failure in America don't explain why black immigrants from Africa and the Caribbean are out-earning and out-succeeding native-born black Americans.

At some point we need to reclaim our responsibility, otherwise nothing will change. All of our social movements are focused on what we expect of other people, but we never look at ourselves to make changes first. We don't see ourselves as capable of change and we are robbing ourselves routinely of this strength. We are acting entitled as we demand that the government and the rest of America cater to us as if we are special. This attitude is making us less accountable and more dependent on the actions of others when we don't need it.

Once you begin to live a life filled with personal responsibility, you will start to see the world differently. You will realize that all the noise that we have actively listened to about some underbelly of oppression that has creeped into every corner of American society and lurks deep into the psyche of white America really doesn't matter. Even when racism was overt and sanctioned by the government, we did what needed to be done to advance as far as possible. We took action to gain our portion even when the world around us was attempting to set us up for failure purely based on our race. So, what is our excuse today?

What I am proposing is difficult, but it is necessary for personal growth and cultural change. My personal journey is only a single example of how accepting responsibility for your failures can lead to a variety of life successes. I no longer carry the burden of being a victim of anxiety, depression, racism, the job market, the dating market, family and a plethora of other issues that I let dictate my happiness. If I were to face discrimination today, it wouldn't bother me because I know that it is their problem, not mine. Why should I interrupt my happiness because someone else holds hate in their heart? Why should I absorb their negative energy when it produces nothing of value?

Personal responsibility does not only involve accepting the consequences of your actions but also being responsible for how you handle your emotions. Experiencing racism, or at least the feeling of being persecuted based on your race, is not pleasant. It's undoubtedly infuriating. But viewing anger as an acceptable response only empowers the person who is inflicting the pain. We love to say that someone made us feel a particular way, but in reality, we each decide to react in a particular way. Things in life are bound to upset us. but it is our choice as to how we will respond to these feelings. I could easily let my emotions get the best of me and then blame my reaction on someone else. Or I can take personal responsibility for how I react.

Once you accept responsibility for your reactions, you will choose wisely which battles you decide to take part in and how you participate in them. I have chosen to conserve my energy so that I only fight for things that may lead to real positive change. It may appear that I don't care about racism but this is false, I just choose not to become overly emotional about the statistically rare and ambiguous situations that involve someone that happens to have a similar complexion to mine. I have chosen to live my life based more on logic and less on emotion because I understand that there are opportunists waiting to prey upon black emotions. I take responsibility for my emotional state and do not allow outside influencers to have power over my internal state of being.

No one can manipulate my emotions unless I give them permission to. Also, no one can use my race to dictate who I am in this world unless I let them. This is the emotional state of the strong willed and the accountable. Black Americans for far too long have been allowing outside actors to play off our emotional sensitivities, allowing opportunists entry into their hearts only to string them along with victim ideology.

I am no longer fearful in life as long as I'm the one making the decisions. If failure is what follows, then I believe in my ability to learn from it to succeed later. I no longer fear that the racist boogeyman is waiting for me. I am done waiting for other people to help me because true leadership means that you must take the first step before everyone else. I don't need handouts or sympathy because of my blackness. I see that as insulting. I don't need socialized shortcuts that imply lowered expectations. I am more than capable of excelling without the help of people with a savior complex.

I am a human being before I am black and the sooner that others realize this, the sooner they will respect me instead of attempting to pity me. I deserve what I have earned, not what I am given. Lastly, I am a descendant of people who overcame because only the strong survive and I choose to live this way in order for my son to view his father's legacy as something to be proud of.

- CHAPTER 25 -

SOLUTION - REALIZE THAT YOU ARE A VICTOR

"Far better is it to dare mighty things, to win glorious triumphs, even though checkered by failure... than to rank with those poor spirits who neither enjoy nor suffer much, because they live in a gray twilight that knows not victory nor defeat."

—Theodore Roosevelt

Do we ask ourselves what America looks like once we've won? What does it mean to be victorious? What if the fight has become more enticing than the actual win itself? What if accepting the win exposes some of our failures? What if our failures are the beginnings of our future achievements?

Black Americans must have a greater perspective on what it actually means to have won. Americans tend to have a skewed perspective of our country compared to the rest of the world. We are only a miniscule population in a greater world that in many places live in overwhelming poverty with openly corrupt governments, economic insecurity, currency that wavers in value, and rare opportunities for upward mobility.

If you are a black American, you have already won. You are the descendant of victorious people that strove for betterment, and you should carry this legacy moving forward with pride, not insecurity. You are also among the most privileged black people in the world and the sooner you can accept this exceptional birthright privilege, the sooner you can begin your journey as a victor.

You can curse the western world, spit on the American flag and wag your finger at your history books, but you are American, and you benefit from all the perks of being an American. There is no perfect nation, there are no perfect people, and there have always been human atrocities. It is an unfortunate part of the human condition. What matters is how we move forward from these wrongs.

We have lost our perspective on how lucky we are to be in such a fortunate position even if some of our history involved very unfortunate events. Either way, we are here, and we are Americans, not Africans. We have every right to be called Americans without a politically correct hyphen attached to describe us. Our ancestor's blood, sweat and tears have seeped into the soil like any other American of the past, making us all brothers and sisters in the same garden. This should give us a desire to see our country grow upward, not apart.

What does winning actually look like for black Americans? Winning means that meritocracy prevails over the insulting nature of affirmative action. Winning means that the government does not prevent us from achieving greatness by offering us dependency. Winning means that we have the freedom to fail and succeed as we choose. Winning means you can live your life based on your individual traits and not on your racial makeup.

Much of black history in America has focused on what others have attempted to do against black people. Racial laws and policies have been used to control the behavior of this nation. Those laws have been gone for decades and the average American views them as a stain on American history that is hard to remove. The fact that we view these situations in such a negative light means that we have won.

Try burning a cross on a black person's lawn and see the vast repercussions that would take place. Try restricting a black person from doing something as mundane as entering a restaurant. See what happens if they are refused service. A flurry of outrage will come. These are all great indicators that we've won.

What isn't winning? Winning isn't American perfection because that is impossible. Winning isn't the eradication of hate. Winning isn't constantly subjugating non-blacks with racial charges due to our own insecurity or sensitivity. Winning isn't retaining the victim mindset as a form of black kinship. Winning isn't having people bend over backwards to appease our sensitivities as though we need shortcuts in life. Winning isn't taking up social causes that create better bumper sticker slogans rather than positive outcomes for black people.

We struggle to see that we've won because people are constantly trying to tell us that we lost hundreds of years ago and to portray our ancestors as being losers. Every time we attempt to pick ourselves up, someone else has their hand out, wanting to lift us up when we have two strong legs. We find it difficult to see that we've won because all we have been educated about is our fight against struggle. We act as if we are war-torn people that haven't been told that the war was over decades ago.

There will always be discrimination and there will always be racism, but the battle for equality in the eyes of the government has been won long ago. The vast majority of American society was convinced long ago that this type of behavior is ill advised and immoral. If the expectation is that we are to experience a sort of kumbaya-like hands across America moment to signify our victory, then I can understand your disappointment because that will never happen, nor does it need to.

Victory for black Americans is a victory for all Americans. To live by the founding principles of America, even if some of the founding fathers didn't, means that we have to start seeing people for who they are rather than what they are. If all men are created equal, then we need to in fact live out these principles. It does America no good if white Americans live immorally with racial hatred in their hearts, and likewise, it benefits no one if black Americans have racial animosity against white Americans.

If we realize that we've won, there is no need to constantly fight invisible forces through social movements. You can be battle ready, but there is a fine line between defensive readiness and offensive pugilism. Today, we are seeking to fight every racial battle, even if the battles are ambiguous in nature. We appear to always be on the offensive when the greater war has long been over. Our predictable pugilism leads us to be manipulated by those who seek to profit off people who believe the war has never ended.

Discontinuing a war that has long been over will make us see how much energy we have wasted in disliking an enemy that isn't necessarily fighting us back. When you are a soldier, those that aren't wearing your uniform are easily perceived as possible enemies, however their outfit does not predict their intent. The enemy that we are seeking has surrendered a long time ago, but we are blind to their waving white flag.

The truth is that we have always had more in common with our so-called enemies than different. The truth is that the racial war has always been used to divide our country to conquer the hearts and minds of the common people. Even in war, someone always profits, and in our war, it hasn't been the average American regardless of race who has benefited. The reality is that this war was manufactured by the same type of people that run the largest government institutions and corporate conglomerates. The war was intended for us to focus on each other rather than those that reign above us. The American people were fighting an illusionary racial war, the elite were fighting an ideological war.

If you can accept the win, then you will start to see some of our visible shortcomings and start to address them. Every culture has experienced some form of failure, but it's not the failures that determine who they are, it's how they react to those failures. We can blame white historical oppression every day with every passing breath, but what does that actually change? If your house burns down, are you willing to sleep in the rubble while crying about the actions of the arsonist, or will you move forward and start rebuilding from the ashes?

We can blame white people from the past, we can blame various political ideologies, and we can blame the government with some justification. But we ultimately were the ones who committed the actions that are degrading black American society today. No white man convinced my father to abandon his fatherly duties. He did it on his own accord. No white man put a gun into the hands of an urban terrorist so he can kill his brethren. He did it freely. No white man forced us to take government money to subsidize our poverty. We did it willingly. We must stop living life as if we don't have agency and are slaves to everyone else's decisions.

We cannot save the world, but we can save ourselves. We are blessed to be born in this country with great opportunities, as long as you are willing to work hard and have a bit of luck along the way. We cannot lose perspective of how fortunate, or dare I say, privileged we are to be

American citizens. There are wonderful countries in this world that are beautiful in their own way. But there is a reason why America has the highest rate of immigration in the world. People from other countries can see that we have something special here, why can't we?

I am optimistic that our failures will not be the end result, but only a hurdle in the marathon called American progress. One must fail to succeed. But to succeed one cannot wish failure on others. We must lean on our morality as a guiding light for our daily living without perversion from politicians, elitists, propagandists and opportunists.

We are only victims if we choose to be. We are victors if we are willing to accept it.

Made in United States
Orlando, FL
23 May 2024

47148896R00174